PROVERBS

Wisdom
for Living

A Guided Discovery for Groups and Individuals

Kevin Perrotta

LOYOLAPRESS.

CHICAGO

LOYOLAPRESS.

3441 N. ASHLAND AVENUE
CHICAGO, ILLINOIS 60657
(800) 621-1008
WWW.LOYOLABOOKS.ORG

Nihil Obstat
Reverend John G. Lodge, S.S.L., S.T.D.
Censor Deputatus
March 26, 2003

Imprimatur
Most Reverend Raymond E. Goedert, M.A., S.T.L., J.C.L.
Vicar General
Archdiocese of Chicago
March 31, 2003

The *Nihil Obstat* and *Imprimatur* are official declarations that a book is free of doctrinal and moral error. No implication is contained therein that those who have granted the *Nihil Obstat* and *Imprimatur* agree with the content, opinions, or statements expressed. Nor do they assume any legal responsibility associated with publication.

Unless otherwise noted, the Scripture quotations contained herein are from the New Revised Standard Version Bible: Catholic Edition, copyright © 1993 and 1989 by the Division of Christian Education of the National Council of the Churches of Christ in the U.S.A. Used by permission. All rights reserved. Subheadings in Scripture quotations have been added by Kevin Perrotta.

More information on Blessed Frédéric Ozanam (p. 37) may be found at the Web site of the St. Vincent de Paul Society (www.ozanet.org).

St. Thomas Aquinas presents his analysis of sloth (p. 69) in his *Summa Theologiae,* "Second Part of the Second Part," question 35. A translation of the *Summa* can be found at the Christian Classics Ethereal Library Web site (www.ccel.org).

More information on Archbishop Oscar Romero (p. 79) may be found in Jon Sobrino, *Archbishop Romero: Memories and Reflections,* Robert R. Barr, trans. (Maryknoll, N.Y.: Orbis Books, 1990); and in Marie Dennis, Renny Golden, and Scott Wright, *Oscar Romero: Reflections on His Life and Writings* (Maryknoll, N.Y.: Orbis Books, 2000).

The quotations from James G. Williams (p. 83) are taken from his book *Those Who Ponder Proverbs* (Sheffield, England: Almond Press, 1981).

The Scripture quotation from the Revised Standard Version (p. 85) is taken from the Revised Standard Version of the Bible, copyright © 1946, 1952, and 1971 by the Division of Christian Education of the National Council of the Churches of Christ in the USA. Used by permission. All rights reserved.

The Scripture quotation from the New International Version of the Bible (p. 85) is taken from the Holy Bible, New International Version®. Copyright © 1973, 1978, 1984 by International Bible Society. Used by permission of Zondervan Publishing House. All rights reserved.

Interior design by Kay Hartmann/Communique Design
Illustration by Charise Mericle Harper

ISBN 0-8294-1567-X

Printed in the United States of America

03 04 05 06 07 08 09 10 Bang 10 9 8 7 6 5 4 3 2 1

Contents

How to Use This Guide

Y ou might compare the Bible to a national park. The park is so large that you could spend months, even years, getting to know it. But a brief visit, if carefully planned, can be enjoyable and worthwhile. In a few hours you can drive through the park and pull over at a handful of sites. At each stop you can get out of the car, take a short trail through the woods, listen to the wind blowing through the trees, get a feel for the place.

In this booklet, we will read portions of the book of Proverbs. Because the excerpts are short, we will be able to take a leisurely walk through them, thinking carefully about what we are reading and what it means for our lives today. Proverbs is a practical book about how to live well, and it offers a great deal for our reflection.

This guide provides everything you need to explore the excerpts from Proverbs in six discussions—or to do a six-part exploration on your own. The introduction on page 6 will prepare you to get the most out of your reading. The weekly sections provide explanations that will help illuminate the meanings of the readings for your life. Equally important, each section supplies questions that will launch your group into fruitful discussion, helping you to both investigate the proverbs for yourself and learn from one another. If you're using the booklet by yourself, the questions will spur your personal reflection.

Each discussion is meant to be a *guided discovery.*

Guided. None of us is equipped to read the Bible without help. We read the Bible *for* ourselves but not *by* ourselves. Scripture was written to be understood and applied in the community of faith. So each week "A Guide to the Reading," drawing on the work of both modern biblical scholars and Christian writers of the past, supplies background and explanations. The guide will help you grasp the meanings of the book of Proverbs. Think of it as a friendly park ranger who points out noteworthy details and explains what you're looking at so you can appreciate things for yourself.

Discovery. The purpose is for *you* to interact with Proverbs. "Questions for Careful Reading" is a tool to help you dig into the text and examine it carefully. "Questions for Application" will help you consider what these words mean for your life here and now. Each week concludes with an "Approach to Prayer" section that helps you respond to God's word. Supplementary "Living Tradition" and "Saints in the Making" sections offer the thoughts and experiences of Christians past and present. By showing what the proverbs have meant to others, these sections will help you consider what they mean for you.

How long are the discussion sessions? We've assumed you will have about an hour and a half when you get together. If you have less time, you'll find that most of the elements can be shortened somewhat.

Is homework necessary? You will get the most out of your discussions if you read the weekly material and prepare answers to the questions in advance of each meeting. If participants are not able to prepare, have someone read the "Guide to the Reading" sections aloud to the group at the points where they appear.

What about leadership? If you happen to have a world-class biblical scholar in your group, by all means ask him or her to lead the discussions. In the absence of any professional Scripture scholars, or even accomplished amateur biblical scholars, you can still have a first-class Bible discussion. Choose two or three people to take turns as facilitators, and have everyone read "Suggestions for Bible Discussion Groups" (page 90) before beginning.

Does everyone need a guide? a Bible? Everyone in the group will need his or her own copy of this booklet. It contains all the texts from Proverbs that are discussed in the weekly sessions, so a Bible is not absolutely necessary—but each participant will find it useful to have one. Some of the questions call for reading passages of Scripture that are not included in this booklet. You should have at least one Bible on hand for your discussions (see page 94 for recommendations.)

How do we get started? Before you begin, take a look at the suggestions for Bible discussion groups (page 90) or individuals (page 93).

First Things First

What's the Use of Proverbs?

In a closet, I have a box of old, black-and-white family photos. Despite good intentions, I have never made much progress in my occasional attempts at organizing them. I start efficiently, putting the pictures in piles according to dates and branches of the family; then something snags my attention. Ah, here's Aunt Ursula as a girl, wearing a lacy dress . . . and here are my stiffly posed great-grandparents on the Cassano side (I have the faintest memory of Granny Cassano as a very old woman). And this is my father as a soldier on leave in Germany at the end of World War II (why, he's so *young*—younger than my own sons are today!). All of them are gone now. What is one to make of their lives? Look at Ursula's eager little face. She seems to think the world has made her great promises. Did it deliver what she expected? What about my great-grandparents? Anthony was in his thirties, Maria Magdalena only fourteen on their wedding day. Were they content with their life together when he died, some thirty years and eight children later? How did the jaunty guy in uniform become the more tired man I knew as Dad? Did they live well? Did they make a success of their lives? I ponder the situations they faced, the choices they made, and where they came out at in the end. Picture sorting ceases. After a while, I gather up the photos and put them back in the box still jumbled together.

Did they make a success of their lives? Probably all of us ask that question about family members and friends who have reached the end of their earthly journey. It is not easy to say *precisely* what the question asks, for undoubtedly each of us would offer a somewhat different definition of success. Yet most of us share a general notion of a life well lived. Making a success of life means using your talents and resources well, meeting challenges constructively, standing by the people who depend on you, putting in more than you take out as you pass through life, ending up more cheerful than embittered. The successful person keeps stupid mistakes to a minimum, steers clear of futile conflicts, and is directed by some inner compass toward what is important.

Did *they* make a success of their lives? Intriguing as the question may be, it is not the most important inquiry for us to pursue. During my occasional photo-organizing sessions, I have gotten the feeling that I am not the only one doing the questioning. Gazing out from their niches in the past, the people in the photos interrogate *me.* "We lived our lives," they say. "What are you doing with yours?"

This is the question that our common spiritual ancestors pose to all of us through the book of Proverbs. Israelite peasants and sages originated and collected the proverbs. Through their book, these long-ago relatives-in-faith lean toward us, pointing their forefingers at each of us in a gesture of challenge: "Make a success of *your* life!" To help us do it, they have given us their book.

The starting point for using their book is to consider what kind of help we need. What goes into the art of living well?

Obviously success in life does not consist of a single act. We succeed or fail in life by the way we live. Essentially, "the way we live" means the choices we make. Life presents us with options; living consists in choosing among them. Successful living is choosing well.

Our choices range from trivial to weighty. Should I put off grocery shopping until Saturday? Should I ask Louise to marry me? Once made, each decision moves us forward into a new situation, where new options open before us, all options leading potentially to further arrays of choices, branching out in various directions. By making choices, we progress from one set of options to another, from moment to moment throughout life.

We make our choices on the basis of what we know and in light of the advice we receive. Of knowledge and guidance there is no shortage of suppliers. Television, print media, and the Web are with us wherever we go. Teachers, trainers, and therapists crowd around us from nursery school to nursing home. But living well requires something more basic than instruction and counsel, for only a certain kind of person makes good and discerning use of these inputs. Only a certain kind of person makes good choices and lives well. What kind of person is that?

The biblical writers offer a picture of the person who is qualified to make a success of life. The person who can succeed in life possesses common sense, upright conscience, self-control, and authentic values. The biblical writers call this package of characteristics *wisdom.* The person who embodies these characteristics is *wise.* The wise person is able to live well.

In short, to make a success of our lives, we must become persons of wisdom. This is where Proverbs comes in. The book is a training program for becoming wise.

The training program in the book of Proverbs consists—no surprise—mostly of proverbs. As we all know, proverbs are brief, memorably phrased observations on life. Every society has its proverbs. They crystallize the experience of the community. Through proverbs, people articulate what they have learned about the art of living. In these pithy sayings, people refine their insights into how the world works and what is worthwhile; they polish them and pass them on, like shiny coins, to the next generation.

But how do proverbs help us to become wise? Does memorizing proverbs—stocking the shelves of our mind with as many of these time-tested insights as possible—make us wise? We certainly need the insights of those who are wiser than we are. But, as we have seen, we need something more basic than other people's insights—even divinely inspired ones. We need to become the kind of people who can use those insights to make good choices in the situations we face. How do proverbs contribute to this process of personal development?

Simply, proverbs spur us to think about life.

Consider the proverb "A rolling stone gathers no moss." This conveys the observation that if you keep moving from place to place, certain experiences, good and bad, will elude you. So should Maria stay in Colorado or move to Michigan? Or what about the biblical proverb "The glory of children is their parents" (17:6—unless noted, all biblical citations in this book refer to Proverbs)? This points up a value: parents deserve recognition. Should Virginia, then, keep her maiden name when she marries Glen? Obviously, proverbs don't answer such questions. By their nature, proverbs are incomplete. A proverb contains an insight but never instructions on how the insight might—or might not—apply to any particular situation.

Paradoxically, the incompleteness of proverbs is what makes them helpful for growing in wisdom. Every proverb beckons us to try to "complete" it—to connect it with a situation. Completing proverbs is a demanding exercise, a workout for the mind and heart. The process of trying to complete a proverb involves discovering the crucial differences between the situations where it would apply and those where it would not. What is the difference between the times when you should "look before you leap" and the times when you had better simply leap? "He who hesitates is lost"—but when is it courting disaster to press ahead without second thoughts?

The exercise of completing proverbs sharpens our ability to size up situations and draw lessons from our experience. It develops our capacity to foresee the consequences of our actions. The proverb "Those who guard their mouths preserve their lives" (13:3) spurs us to reflect on *how* shooting off your mouth can get you in trouble. This sort of reasoning impresses on us the importance of asking the right questions before making decisions. It gives us practice in thinking situations through before taking action. It reminds us of the importance of staying calm and using good judgment rather than acting on impulse—and this is an aspect of character development.

Completing proverbs leads us into a consideration of *why* good courses of action have beneficial results—and this is an aspect of conscience development. The proverb "Better is a dinner of vegetables where love is than a fatted ox and hatred with it" (15:17) provokes us to consider *why* human well-being is better fostered by harmony between people than by envy and rivalry. In this way, completing proverbs deepens our commitment to the values that make life good.

Thus completing proverbs can sharpen our perceptiveness, mold our habits of thought, strengthen our devotion to what is good. Of course, we can't become wise *just* by pondering proverbs, any more than a football team can have a successful season just by practicing and working out. But it helps.

The editors of Proverbs have facilitated our pondering of individual proverbs by declining to arrange them in any observable order. The book's proverb collection—chapters 10 through 30—lists some thirty sayings per chapter with little if any detectable scheme. Meeting hundreds of miscellaneous proverbs one after the other is overwhelming. Reading these chapters is like walking around in a hardware store where the entire inventory, from roofing nails to chain saws, has been strewn about on the floor.

The scattershot display of proverbs in Proverbs frustrates the reader's attempts to find themes for reflection. A topical arrangement would have helped the reader to focus on one subject at a time—on money, childrearing, anger, or whatever. Another Old Testament "wisdom" book—the book of Sirach—does, in fact, group proverbs by topics. Yet there is a benefit in the lack of arrangement in the book of Proverbs. Failing to find groupings of proverbs on particular topics, the reader gravitates to single proverbs that catch his or her attention. Thus the reader ends up trying to complete individual proverbs rather than studying topics.

The book's seemingly random amalgamation of proverbs has another hidden advantage. Proverbs are observations on how life goes; they identify regularities in life. Yet life is shot through with the unusual. All observations of pattern and order in the world must be qualified by the acknowledgment of paradoxes. The jumble of proverbs in the book of Proverbs reflects this unsystematic character of life. It conveys a more realistic impression of the world than an orderly classification might. By aiding us in seeing the normal patterns in life, the study of proverbs carries the danger of leading us to feel as though we are coming to master the world and learn formulas for dealing with it successfully. The randomness of the proverb collection steers us away from such illusions.

It is useful to know something about the authors and original readers of the biblical books. This information can help us discover the books' messages and avoid misunderstandings. In many cases, however, the identities and situations of the biblical authors and their audiences are shadowy. The book of Proverbs is one of these cases.

Most scholars do agree in offering a general view of the process by which Proverbs came into existence. Many of the proverbs in the book originated as folk sayings in ancient Israelite society. At some point, more educated people—often referred to as sages—collected the sayings, adding some of their own. The sages may have begun their work as early as the time of David and Solomon, a millennium before Jesus. They may have worked at the royal court. Jews who returned from exile in Babylon in the fifth century before Christ may have completed the earlier sages' work by composing the introductory and concluding chapters (chapters 1–9 and 31), which they wrapped around the proverb collection itself (chapters 10–30). But beyond this rather indistinct picture of the book's origins, there is little certain information that might guide us in its interpretation.

Fortunately, knowing about authors and setting is less important in reading Proverbs than in reading some other biblical writings. The prophetic books, for example, were addressed to particular people in particular historical situations. To the extent that we cannot ascertain those situations, we remain somewhat in the dark about the books' original meanings. Individual proverbs, however, are observations extracted from the particular situations in which they arose. The particular situations in which they originated are thus no longer important for grasping their meaning. Proverbs are generalizations, designed to apply to a wide variety of situations—including our own.

In many ways, Proverbs is an optimistic book. The proverbs imply confidence in the innate human capacity to become wise, that is, to become the kind of person who can make a success of life. Proverbs are evidence that people can learn from their experiences. Thus the proverbs implicitly encourage us to do what their authors did: to open our eyes, to pay attention to how the world works, to reflect on our experiences, to learn from our mistakes. If our spiritual ancestors were able to gain wisdom, well, so can we! The mere existence of this collection of ordinary people's proverbs in the Bible is an invitation to us to enter into the proverb-making process—to learn about life and pass on what we learn.

By their origin in ordinary people's lives, proverbs point to the everyday world as the arena where wisdom is acquired. While formal education and training play a role in our personal development, the proverbs suggest that we become wise by going through our own trial-and-error learning in the process of living, just as the proverb writers did.

Wisdom must be discovered anew by each individual—and can be. Just as God was with the ordinary people who encapsulated their observations on life in the proverbs that ended up in the Bible, so he is with each of us as we attempt to complete the proverbs by applying them to our world today—and learn from our own experiences.

This is not to say, however, that the proverbs are an encouragement to individualism. Through proverbs one generation crystallizes what it has learned and passes it on to the next. The mere fact that sages collected proverbs testifies to their conviction that learning from others is essential for growing in wisdom. While each of us must search for wisdom for ourselves, we must search for it not only in our own raw experience but also in the insights acquired by previous generations.

The overall structure of the book of Proverbs brings out the interplay between learning for ourselves and learning from the community of faith. The first nine chapters of the book are lectures by an older person to a younger one, the older urging the younger to set out on the path toward wisdom. The proverbs themselves (chapters 10 through 30) are the content of the program—the textbook for the course. By themselves, proverbs encourage individual reflection on one's own experience. By incorporating the proverbs into a program of instruction, however, the editors have highlighted the importance of learning from those who are wiser. (This may spur us to consider whether we have found wise men and women to help us learn to make a success of our lives.)

While the proverbs stimulate us to observe the world for ourselves, the book of Proverbs does not offer them as mere opinions—suggestions that the learner is free to disregard. The opening chapters (1–9), in which we hear the voices of older, wiser teachers, introduce the proverbs as elements of authoritative instruction (2:1; 3:1). Thus, while individual proverbs invite our pondering, we are invited to ponder where and how they might be completed in particular situations, not whether they are valid. In any society, the older folk hand on proverbs authoritatively as expressions of the community's cultural tradition. In the case of Proverbs, the community's tradition is especially authoritative because it reflects the learning of a community that has been living in covenant with God. The tradition of this community, Israel, communicates how to live as God wills.

The book of Proverbs, then, while encouraging us to learn both from our own experience and from the experience of others, points us toward God as the ultimate source of wisdom. God is the one who enables us to become persons who possess common sense, upright conscience, self-control, and authentic values. Only with God's help can we become wise and put our wisdom to good use. The sages who composed Proverbs emphasize that successful living arises from a relationship with God and culminates in intimacy with God. The book communicates this point in a poetic manner by picturing God's wisdom as a wise woman who welcomes the (presumably male) learner to her house to share a meal with her and, ultimately, to marry her and enjoy the benefits of life with her.

For the sages, wisdom is the path for succeeding in this world in ordinary, tangible ways—prospering materially, raising a happy family, achieving recognition for service to the community. Yet wisdom, in essence, is companionship with God. In this sense, wisdom itself is worth far more than all the benefits it brings (3:13–15; 8:10–11; 20:15). While wisdom concerns how to do mundane things well, it raises our eyes to God as the goal of our lives. At the same time, because the proverbs concern the ordinary, everyday world, they imply that we encounter the God-who-makes-wise in the ordinary hours of our lives.

Other Old Testament "wisdom" books—Job, Ecclesiastes, Sirach, Wisdom of Solomon—further explore the mysteries of wisdom. Finally, wisdom receives its definitive treatment in the New Testament, where we encounter Jesus of Nazareth. He is the wisdom of God in person. Discipleship to him is the essence of wise living. Jesus moves the wisdom of the Old Testament to a higher level—a subject touched on in an essay at the end of this book ("Saving the Best Till Last: Jesus, Speaker of Proverbs," page 84).

A final editorial note before we begin: the article "Make Haste Slowly!: Cracking Open the Proverbs" (page 24) offers practical suggestions for how to get the most out of your reading of individual proverbs. I recommend reading it before you begin the reading for week 2.

WELL BEGUN IS HALF DONE

Questions to Begin

15 minutes
Use a question or two to get warmed up for the reading.

1 What sorts of things do you find it easy to remember? to forget?

2 When was the last time you raised your voice in conversation or to make a request?

5 minutes
Read the passage aloud. Let individuals take turns reading sections.

The Reading: Proverbs 2:1–11; 3:1–18

The Teacher's Assurances

1 My child, if you accept my words
 and treasure up my commandments within you,
2 making your ear attentive to wisdom
 and inclining your heart to understanding;
3 if you indeed cry out for insight,
 and raise your voice for understanding;
4 if you seek it like silver,
 and search for it as for hidden treasures—
5 then you will understand the fear of the LORD
 and find the knowledge of God.
6 For the LORD gives wisdom;
 from his mouth come knowledge and understanding;
7 he stores up sound wisdom for the upright;
 he is a shield to those who walk blamelessly,
8 guarding the paths of justice
 and preserving the way of his faithful ones.
9 Then you will understand righteousness and justice
 and equity, every good path;
10 for wisdom will come into your heart,
 and knowledge will be pleasant to your soul;
11 prudence will watch over you;
 and understanding will guard you.

The Learner's Attitudes

3:1 My child, do not forget my teaching,
 but let your heart keep my commandments;
2 for length of days and years of life
 and abundant welfare they will give you.

3 Do not let loyalty and faithfulness forsake you;
 bind them around your neck,
 write them on the tablet of your heart.
4 So you will find favor and good repute
 in the sight of God and of people.

5 Trust in the LORD with all your heart,
    and do not rely on your own insight.
6 In all your ways acknowledge him,
    and he will make straight your paths.
7 Do not be wise in your own eyes;
    fear the LORD, and turn away from evil.
8 It will be a healing for your flesh
    and a refreshment for your body.
9 Honor the LORD with your substance
    and with the first fruits of all your produce;
10 then your barns will be filled with plenty,
    and your vats will be bursting with wine.

11 My child, do not despise the LORD's discipline
    or be weary of his reproof,
12 for the LORD reproves the one he loves,
    as a father the son in whom he delights.

The Attractiveness of the Goal

13 Happy are those who find wisdom,
    and those who get understanding,
14 for her income is better than silver,
    and her revenue better than gold.
15 She is more precious than jewels,
    and nothing you desire can compare with her.
16 Long life is in her right hand;
    in her left hand are riches and honor.
17 Her ways are ways of pleasantness,
    and all her paths are peace.
18 She is a tree of life to those who lay hold of her;
    those who hold her fast are called happy.

10 minutes
Choose questions according to your interest and time.

1 Verses 2:5 and 2:9 speak of the effects of wisdom. What do the two verses have in common? In light of 2:9, what might it mean in 2:5 to "understand the fear of the Lord"?

2 From what kinds of dangers do 2:7–8 promise protection?

3 Verses 2:8 and 2:11 are parallel (the Hebrew words for *guarding* and *preserving* in verse 8 are repeated in verse 11). Who guards and preserves in 2:8? Who guards and preserves in 2:11? What does the parallel imply?

4 Identify references to path, way, road, and walking. How is life like a journey? If life is a journey, what is wisdom?

5 What does it mean to "be wise in your own eyes" (3:7), based on the context (3:5–7)? How can you tell if you are becoming "wise in your own eyes"?

A Guide to the Reading

If participants have not read this section already, read it aloud.
Otherwise go on to "Questions for Application."

Our reading consists of a teacher's speeches to a student. The form is that of counsel from a father to his son, but it expresses equally well what a mother or other older person might wish to say to any young person.

The speaker invites the learner to enter a program of instruction in how to live. For the young person, this means heading toward an unfamiliar goal. "Knowledge" is not yet "pleasant" to the young person (2:10). He or she has not experienced enough of life to know what is truly desirable. Only by gaining wisdom will he or she come to appreciate it. At the outset, then, the young person has to trust the teacher's assurances that the goal is worth the effort. Anyone who took music lessons as a child can understand the learner's situation.

At the beginning, the learner is not expected to understand the path but to simply pay attention to the teacher ("inclining your heart"—2:2). The first stage is to absorb ("accept my words"—2:1). Yet the learner needs to be active, not passive—desiring wisdom, even if he or she does not yet fully grasp what it is (2:3–4).

The next stage involves reflection. The textbook for the course consists of proverbs (chapters 10–30), and these are not only to be memorized but also to be pondered—and put into practice. One comes to understand proverbs about diligence and laziness, for example, by working hard and comparing the results with what happens when one slacks off. The young person needs to grab hold of what is taught ("keep my commandments"—3:1).

"Do not forget my teaching" (3:1), the instructor implores. Don't let it go in one ear and out the other. The instructor's urging to "write *them* on the tablet of your heart" (3:3; emphasis added) probably refers to his "commandments." In other words, the student should engrave the instructions in his or her memory. The teaching should become a permanent part of the learner's character. He or she should become honest, faithful to obligations, hardworking, self-controlled, not taken in by appearances and smooth talk.

Amid all this effort, the learner needs a relationship with God. "In all your ways acknowledge him" (3:6), that is, recognize God as the source of all—a recognition expressed by offerings from the harvest (3:9–10). Depend on God, admitting that you cannot know the outcome of all your acts and do not have the power to make life everything that you want it to be (3:5). Trust that God is wise and good even when he chooses to work through disappointments and sorrows; view problems and sufferings as opportunities to turn from sin and grow to maturity (3:11–12). Follow God's instructions for living (3:7).

The starting point for gaining wisdom is "fear of the Lord" (1:7); the end point is to "understand the fear of the Lord" (2:5; see page 38). At first, the young person obeys God because of fear of punishment. Gradually he or she becomes able to reason about right and wrong. The learner comes to see *why* what is right is right; he or she becomes committed to it on the basis of understanding. Thus the learner develops that built-in moral compass called conscience.

The instructor does not suggest that the road to wisdom is easy. He does, however, assure the beginner that attainment is possible, because God is on the road. God gives wisdom to all who make the effort to receive it (2:6–8). So the young person should be confident. As a later, greater teacher would say, "Search, and you will find" (Matthew 7:7).

The instructor promises that wisdom will bring riches (3:10). By itself, this might seem simplistic, even crass. Yet wisdom herself is better than the benefits she brings (3:13–15). And the teacher guarantees not that the road to wisdom will be strewn with jackpots and bonuses but that God will help the one who steps out on this road to stay on it (2:8). A life wisely lived leads ultimately not to wealth but to God: "Then you will . . . find the knowledge of God" (2:5).

The reading challenges each of us to ask ourselves: Am I (still) a learner? Am I willing to see myself in the young person who needs instruction? The wise person realizes how small his or her flashlight of insight is—and learns to trust God in everything that lies outside its little circle of illumination (3:5). Am I wise enough to be a seeker of wisdom? If so, how should I translate my desire into action?

Questions for Application

40 minutes
Choose questions according to your interest and time.

1 A friend of mine quotes a proverb from his grandfather: "Sometimes wisdom comes with age, but sometimes age comes all by itself." Do people become wiser as they grow older? Why?

2 What helps you to acknowledge God (3:6) throughout the day? How else might you remind yourself of God's presence?

3 What qualities in parents and teachers make it easier for young people to trust them and take seriously what they say?

4 In what ways does our culture train young people to respect old people and their wisdom? In what ways does it encourage young people to think independently and develop their own opinions? Is there a tension between these two attitudes in our society?

5 At the beginning, the learner has to take it on faith that the journey toward wisdom is worth the effort. In what ways do we have to take it on faith that Christian life is worth the effort? Who are the teachers we should trust as we travel the path of Christian life?

6 Describe someone you know (or knew) whom you would call wise. What are the signs of wisdom in this person's life? What impact has this person had on you?

7 The reading calls wisdom "a tree of life" (3:18). The first humans lost access to an earlier "tree of life" (Genesis 2:9; 3:22–24). What might the promise of 3:13–18 mean in relation to the events in Genesis 2–3? There is also a later "tree" in the Bible— the cross on which Jesus died (Acts 5:30). What relationship might there be between this later "tree" and the tree in Proverbs 3:18?

A gentle tongue is a tree of life.

Proverbs 15:4

Approach to Prayer

15 minutes
Use this approach—or create your own!

◆ Pray together this prayer to the Holy Spirit for wisdom. Allow an opportunity for anyone to offer a spontaneous prayer. End with an Our Father and a Glory to the Father.

Speaker: Come, Holy Spirit, fill the hearts of your faithful and enkindle in them the fire of your love. "Send forth your Spirit and they shall be created, and you shall renew the face of the earth."*
Let us pray—

Group: O God, who by the light of the Holy Spirit did instruct the hearts of your faithful, grant that we, by the same Holy Spirit, may be truly wise and ever rejoice in his consolation, through Christ our Lord. Amen.

*Psalm 104:30 (traditional translation)

Living Tradition

A Kindly Educator

This section is a supplement for individual reading.

In our reading from Proverbs this week, the speaker lays out a program of development for the young learner. The student is to advance from inexperience to an understanding of the world, from inability to recognize what is good to mature conscience and character. Over the centuries, many teachers in the Christian tradition have played important roles in the development of educational approaches that help young people achieve these goals. An especially notable figure in this tradition is an Italian priest named John Bosco (1815–88).

The nineteenth century was a time of economic change and social dislocation in northern Italy. In the city of Turin, poor boys, many with little or no family life or adult supervision, crowded the streets—and the growing system of jails. Don Bosco, as he is usually called, devoted himself to meeting these boys' material, spiritual, and educational needs.

Don Bosco's efforts led to the development of a new religious order of men—the Salesians—who operated a system of orphanages and schools for boys in Italy and other countries. A parallel order of women, the Salesian Sisters, grew up under the leadership of one of Don Bosco's colleagues, Mary Mazzarello.

In an age when education tended to emphasize regimentation and punishment, Don Bosco took a different approach. He called it the "preventive system," in contrast to the "repressive system." Don Bosco stressed the importance of the teacher becoming familiar with his or her students—an approach that he exemplified by his constant presence among the boys in his orphanages and schools. By being present among young people not only in the classroom and workshop but also on the playground and during recreational, sports, and cultural activities, Don Bosco found it possible to guide them in a friendly, individualized way and to steer them away from situations that would be harmful to their development. He found that more could be accomplished by treating boys with respect and appealing to them with entertainment, humor, theater, and music than with strict discipline and reliance on punishments. Don Bosco said his system was "wholly based on the words of St. Paul: 'Love is patient and kind; it bears all things, hopes all things, and endures all things'" (see 1 Corinthians 13:4–7).

Between Discussions

Make Haste Slowly!

Cracking Open the Proverbs

Aproverb is wisdom in a nutshell. How do you get at it? Careful reading is the nutcracker. Asking the right questions is the pointy tool for extracting the meat. Here are some suggestions to help you increase your reading skill and some questions that may aid your reflections.

Suggestions for reading. Not every proverb in the world has two parts, although many do ("A place for everything, and everything in its place"). It is, however, the case that almost all the proverbs in the book of Proverbs have two parts: "A soft answer turns away wrath, but a harsh word stirs up anger" (15:1). A tip for reading the proverbs is this: examine the two parts closely so as to understand how they work together.

Sometimes, as in the soft-answer proverb, the relationship is fairly obvious: the two parts are opposites. Together they imply that sometimes we face an either-or choice: we can either say something that will inflame the situation or speak in a way that brings peace.

Often, however, the relationship between the two parts of a proverb is not quite so simple. For example, in some proverbs where the two parts form a contrast, the parts are not balanced opposites: "By insolence the heedless make strife, but wisdom is with those who take advice" (13:10). The two parts contrast those who refuse to heed advice and those who take it—which is simple enough. But insolence and wisdom are not balanced opposites. The opposite of insolence is respect; the opposite of wisdom is foolishness. By setting insolence in contrast to wisdom, the proverb implies that insolence is foolish and respect is wise. Thus the proverb leads us to consider what is foolish about insolence and what is wise about respecting other people. (Try this kind of analysis on two other proverbs in chapter 13—verses 17 and 20).

Some proverbs express similarities rather than contrasts: "It is not right to be partial to the guilty, or to subvert the innocent in judgment" (18:5). Again, however, the parallel between the first and second parts may be altered in a thought-provoking way. "Those with good sense are slow to anger, and it is their glory to overlook an offense" (19:11). Here there is a progression: in the face of an offense, keeping your temper under control shows ordinary common sense; *pardoning* an offense is extraordinary and deserves special praise.

Sometimes the two parts of a proverb help to explain each other: "Desire without knowledge is not good, and one who moves too hurriedly misses the way" (19:2). Here the second part gives an illustration of the first part: a person who knows where they want to go but not how to get there (part one) may set off in a hurry and take the wrong road (part two). Also, the first part helps to explain the second part: the reason why someone might rush off on the wrong road (part two) is that they are acting on impulse without taking time to get the information they need (part one).

Occasionally the second part of a proverb brings the first part to a conclusion: "Laziness brings on deep sleep; an idle person will suffer hunger" (19:15). Laziness leads to inactivity; inactivity leads to an empty refrigerator.

Or the second part of a proverb may intensify the first: "House and wealth are inherited from parents, but a prudent wife is from the Lord" (19:14). Here the second part heightens the first in a couple of ways. First, it indicates that a spouse is more valuable than property. And second, while the first part does not deny the need for God, the second part emphasizes that a person who seeks a good spouse is dependent on God's help. This, in turn, implies something about our ability to find the happiness we seek even in less important departments of life. After all, who chose our parents for us?

At times the second part of the proverb is something of a surprise: "One who loves transgression loves strife; one who builds a high threshold invites broken bones" (17:19). Go figure! In some cases (this one is an example), the surprise in the second part may stem from the translators' inability to understand the Hebrew text.

Questions. Each of our weekly sessions has three sets of questions—Questions to Begin, Questions for Careful Reading, and Questions for Application. These will help you pick the meat out of the proverbial nutshells. As a supplement—or even as an alternative—to the questions in weeks 2, 3, 4, and 5, consider the following questions. These questions will work best if participants prepare their answers ahead of time for the following session.

Questions to begin. To get the most out of the biblical proverbs, you may find it helpful to work a bit with nonbiblical proverbs. Ask each person to come up with a couple of proverbs that are not from the Bible. As you begin the session, go around and give each person a chance to recite one of his or her proverbs. If it is in a different language ("I heard this from my Swedish grandfather . . ."), ask the person to recite it in that language and then give an English translation. (Often proverbs sound better in their original language, even to a person who does not know the language.) Then have the person present his or her answers to the following questions:

◆ Where did you learn the proverb?
◆ What do you find appealing (or annoying!) about it?
◆ Has this proverb guided you?
◆ Has it taken on new or deeper meaning over time?
◆ Have you ever quoted it to others?
◆ Would this proverb fit in the Bible? Why or why not?

If there is time, go around again, letting participants present a second proverb.

Questions for careful reading.

◆ Find two proverbs in the week's reading that are similar. What are the similarities? What are the differences?
◆ Pick any proverb in the reading and determine to whom it is directed.
◆ Do any two proverbs seem in some way to be opposed to each other (for example, 13:12 and 13:19)?
◆ Pick a proverb that seems trite or obvious. Can you find a deeper level of meaning in it or suggest a situation in which someone might wish to quote it?
◆ Identify two or more proverbs in the reading that deal with a common theme. How do these proverbs bring out different aspects of the theme?
◆ Do any of the proverbs express a view that you are surprised to find in the Bible? What is surprising about them? How might you explain why they are in the Bible?
◆ Do any of the proverbs sound like something that an older person in your family says or used to say?

- ◆ Do any of the proverbs express a view that is also expressed in a modern proverb? (Example: The Bible: "Those who guard their mouths preserve their lives"—13:3. World War II: "Loose lips sink ships.") Can you think of a contemporary proverb that runs counter to any of the proverbs in the reading? (The Bible: "Whoever heeds instruction is on the path to life"—10:17. Today: "Different strokes for different folks.")
- ◆ Make up a story in which a character uses one of the proverbs. For a simple example, see how someone took the proverb in 6:10–11 and set it into a ministry in 24:30–34.
- ◆ Take the first part of a proverb and give it a new second part.

Questions for application. Ask each person to choose three or four proverbs from the reading and prepare answers to the following questions. Then go around and ask each person to present his or her answers for one of the chosen proverbs.

- ◆ Why did you choose this proverb? What do you like—or dislike—about it?
- ◆ Very briefly describe a situation in your life where this proverb would have been an appropriate observation or piece of advice. Would you have done better if you had remembered this proverb?
- ◆ What value does the proverb implicitly or explicitly communicate? How important is this value to you?
- ◆ What does this proverb explicitly or implicitly advise a person to do? to avoid?
- ◆ How might this proverb apply to your life at present?

Give an opportunity for others in the group to ask the person a question or two about his or her answers or to offer their own reflections on the proverb. As participants take turns, they should avoid repeating proverbs that other participants have already presented. Continue to go around for as long as you have time.

Between sessions. Keep a record of any nonbiblical proverbs you discover and those biblical proverbs that you focus on in the Questions for Application, along with your reflections on the readings and the discussions. Include proverbs that others introduce and add your reflections. Collect and reflect on proverbs on topics that interest you.

LIVE AND LEARN

Questions to Begin

15 minutes
Use a question or two to get warmed up for the reading. See also the questions on pages 25–27.

1 When have you missed out on an opportunity by talking instead of acting?

2 Describe an incident that has made you more cautious.

5 minutes
Read the passage aloud. You may wish to ask participants to take turns reading individual verses.

The Reading: Proverbs 14

Miscellaneous Proverbs

1 The wise woman builds her house,
  but the foolish tears it down with her own hands.
2 Those who walk uprightly fear the LORD,
  but one who is devious in conduct despises him.
3 The talk of fools is a rod for their backs,
  but the lips of the wise preserve them.
4 Where there are no oxen, there is no grain;
  abundant crops come by the strength of the ox.
5 A faithful witness does not lie,
  but a false witness breathes out lies.
6 A scoffer seeks wisdom in vain,
  but knowledge is easy for one who understands.
7 Leave the presence of a fool,
  for there you do not find words of knowledge.
8 It is the wisdom of the clever to understand where they go,
  but the folly of fools misleads.
9 Fools mock at the guilt offering,
  but the upright enjoy God's favor.
10 The heart knows its own bitterness,
  and no stranger shares its joy.
11 The house of the wicked is destroyed,
  but the tent of the upright flourishes.
12 There is a way that seems right to a person,
  but its end is the way to death.
13 Even in laughter the heart is sad,
  and the end of joy is grief.
14 The perverse get what their ways deserve,
  and the good, what their deeds deserve.
15 The simple believe everything,
  but the clever consider their steps.
16 The wise are cautious and turn away from evil,
  but the fool throws off restraint and is careless.
17 One who is quick-tempered acts foolishly,
  and the schemer is hated.

18 The simple are adorned with folly,
   but the clever are crowned with knowledge.
19 The evil bow down before the good,
   the wicked at the gates of the righteous.
20 The poor are disliked even by their neighbors,
   but the rich have many friends.
21 Those who despise their neighbors are sinners,
   but happy are those who are kind to the poor.
22 Do they not err that plan evil?
   Those who plan good find loyalty and faithfulness.
23 In all toil there is profit,
   but mere talk leads only to poverty.
24 The crown of the wise is their wisdom,
   but folly is the garland of fools.
25 A truthful witness saves lives,
   but one who utters lies is a betrayer.
26 In the fear of the LORD one has strong confidence,
   and one's children will have a refuge.
27 The fear of the LORD is a fountain of life,
   so that one may avoid the snares of death.
28 The glory of a king is a multitude of people;
   without people a prince is ruined.
29 Whoever is slow to anger has great understanding,
   but one who has a hasty temper exalts folly.
30 A tranquil mind gives life to the flesh,
   but passion makes the bones rot.
31 Those who oppress the poor insult their Maker,
   but those who are kind to the needy honor him.
32 The wicked are overthrown by their evildoing,
   but the righteous find a refuge in their integrity.
33 Wisdom is at home in the mind of one who has
      understanding,
   but it is not known in the heart of fools.
34 Righteousness exalts a nation,
   but sin is a reproach to any people.
35 A servant who deals wisely has the king's favor,
   but his wrath falls on one who acts shamefully.

10 minutes
Choose questions according to your interest and time. See also the questions on pages 25–27.

1 What message might be obtained by putting 14:11 and 14:12 together? by putting 14:12 and 14:13 together?

2 Do any of the proverbs describe a state of affairs that the proverb writer may not approve of?

3 In what way might 14:34 be read as a qualification of 14:28?

4 Some proverbs contrast wisdom with foolishness; others contrast uprightness with doing evil. How does 14:1, on wisdom and foolishness, shed light on 14:11, on wickedness and uprightness? What does the contrast of foolishness and uprightness in 14:9 suggest about the relationship between uprightness and wisdom?

5 What is the point of the first part of 14:24?

A Guide to the Reading

If participants have not read this section already, read it aloud. Otherwise go on to "Questions for Application."

14:1. The woman pulling her house apart stone by stone is a vivid metaphor for a person who neglects his or her talents, squanders money, misses opportunities, destroys trust, alienates family and friends.

14:2. This proverb helps to answer questions such as "In practice, what does it mean to fear the Lord?" and "How can I know whether I do?"

14:3. The first line of this proverb reads literally "the talk of fools is a rod of pride"—the point being, perhaps, that foolish people are verbally aggressive. Part two, then, may assert that sensible people know how to defend themselves against foolish accusations.

14:4. This proverb may also be translated: "When there are no oxen, the feeding trough is empty." Getting rid of your farm animals makes for a tidy, trouble-free barn, but profitable farming involves messiness and hard work. (And what about successful childrearing?)

14:5. This proverb seems obvious (like 14:25). Maybe it is an encouragement to accept the report of a person who is a known truth-teller and to reject the report of a known liar.

14:6. The person who lacks respect for other people cannot find wisdom, even if he or she seeks it. (Why is that?)

14:8. Part one declares that wisdom calculates the possible effects of an action. But part two points out that we can be deceived about the likely outcome of our acts. By whom are we misled? See 14:15—and 14:12!

14:9. Puzzled? Relax. This proverb in Hebrew is as difficult to explain as it is in English.

14:10. A proverb to keep in mind the next time you're tempted to tell a suffering person, "I know how you feel."

14:11–12. The proverb in 14:11 is optimistic about the benefits of doing what is right (like 14:14, 32). But 14:12 points to the limit to which any individual can discern what is right, thus spurring us to seek advice from others. Perhaps 14:12 also reminds us of the limits of all human wisdom. All the wisdom in the world can never entirely grasp the complexities of a situation or foresee all the possible outcomes of an action.

14:13. Like 14:10, the first part of this proverb cautions us against making hasty assessments of other people's states of mind and heart.

14:16. The fool is "careless," literally "trusting": he or she is confident, that is, self-confident. Self-confidence is fine up to a point, beyond which it becomes dangerous. Where is that point? (How can you know whether you've exceeded it?)

14:17. Short-tempered people make fools of themselves, which is bad enough. Even worse, calculating people make themselves hated.

14:19. "The gates" here are probably those of a wealthy person's house. The proverb envisions evildoers having to beg at a just person's front door. Did the rich man in one of Jesus' parables (Luke 16:19–31) feel free to disregard the needy man at his gate because he misunderstood this proverb and concluded that a beggar *must* be a sinner? (Does this mentality operate today?)

14:20–21. The situation observed in the first proverb is sharply criticized in the second. The basis for the criticism is expressed in 14:31. Part two of 14:21 would fit among the "blessed" statements Jesus makes in the Sermon on the Mount (Matthew 5:3–11).

14:23. While the poor should be shown kindness (14:21–22), we are reminded that some poverty stems from lack of effort.

14:24. More literally, part two reads: "the foolishness of fools is foolishness." Unlike the wise, fools don't have anything that could even remotely be compared to a sign of distinction (no "crown," or wreath). All they have is folly.

14:26–27. On "the fear of the Lord," see page 38.

14:28. Ancient governments did not pursue population-control policies.

14:29. The theme of self-control runs throughout the proverbs.

14:30. In the Hebrew, it is clear that the "passion" that eats away at a person's bones is *envy*.

14:31. Here is the basis for an entire social ethic.

14:34. This might also be translated: "Righteousness exalts a people, but a people's strength [exalts] sin!" Thus it would be a warning to any powerful nation not to fall into arrogance.

Questions for Application

40 minutes
Choose questions according to your interest and time. See also the
questions on pages 25–27.

1 Reread the first part of 14:5.
Describe a situation in which
you believed (or failed to
believe) someone whom you
knew to be honest when they
said something that was hard
to believe. What did you learn
from this experience?

2 Refer back to the comments on
14:6 in the Guide to the
Reading. How would you answer
the question there?

3 When have you felt the truth of
14:10? How has this affected
how you relate to other people?

4 How accurate are the assessments of how the world works in 14:11, 14, and 19? How useful are generalizations such as these?

5 Why is rottenness (14:30) an apt metaphor for envy?

6 In your experience, what is the relationship between wisdom and uprightness? between folly and sin?

Iron sharpens iron, and one person sharpens the wits of another.

Proverbs 27:17

Approach to Prayer

15 minutes
Use this approach—or create your own!

◆ Begin with an Our Father. Then pray Psalm 34, which speaks of "the fear of the Lord" (Psalm 34:11)—a topic touched on in this week's reading (14:2, 26, 27). If not everyone in the group has the same translation of the Bible, ask one person with a Bible to read the whole psalm aloud, slowly. End with a Glory to the Father.

Note: Next week's Approach to Prayer (page 48) suggests a way of praying that will work best if participants have prepared for it. If you plan to use it, read it aloud now so that group members may reflect on it in preparation for the next meeting.

Saints in the Making

From the Abstract to the Personal

This section is a supplement for individual reading.

T hose who oppress the poor insult their Maker, but those who are kind to the needy honor him" (14:31).

Newly recommitted to Christianity after a period of adolescent doubt, eighteen-year-old Frédéric Ozanam arrived in Paris in 1831 wanting to see the gospel brought to bear on the problems created by the industrial revolution. The young law student was particularly troubled by the indignity suffered by factory workers. "It is exploitation," Ozanam wrote to a friend, "when the owner considers the worker not as an associate or an assistant but as a tool of production." It is the Church's mission, he wrote, to bring to workers "the indestructible awareness of their dignity as persons." While his social concern was genuine, however, the scholarly Ozanam moved largely in the realm of ideas.

The following year, Ozanam helped to organize a discussion club where believers and nonbelievers wrangled over literary and religious topics—an activity in which Ozanam excelled. But eventually the intellectual sparring wearied him. He felt the need to move beyond mere controversy. With half a dozen student friends, Ozanam launched another group. Rather than arguing about Christianity, they intended to show nonbelievers its value by serving the poor. But just what were these young, comfortably middle-class intellectuals, who did not know any poor people, going to do?

The answer came into view when the group consulted Sister Rosalie. A member of a religious order called the Daughters of Charity, she lived in a Paris slum and worked tirelessly to alleviate the sufferings of homeless people, alcoholics, abandoned children, and destitute families. Sister Rosalie put the young men to work visiting the poor in their homes, bringing them bread and firewood and getting to know them personally. Ozanam immediately felt he had found his vocation.

The group took one of the founders of Sister Rosalie's order, St. Vincent de Paul, as their model. As the St. Vincent de Paul Society, the group expanded rapidly into a network of Catholics who worked to identify and care for their neediest neighbors. By the time Ozanam died in 1853, thousands of Catholics were serving in the society. Today more than half a million men and women are active in it in 132 countries.

Between Discussions

Square One

The Fear of the Lord

T hree proverbs in the reading in week 2 speak about the fear of the Lord (14:2, 26, 27). What is it?

In the Bible, fear of the Lord is, first of all, literally fear of God, in the sense of awe. For example, the psalmist expresses this fear when he marvels at God's power displayed in a storm sweeping in from the sea (Psalm 29). Jesus' disciples felt it when they caught a glimpse of his heavenly glory in a mountaintop experience. "They were terrified," Mark reports (Mark 9:6). Fear of the Lord is not fear that God wishes us ill or comes to harm us. It is simply an overwhelming sense of the immense disproportion between the Almighty and our little selves.

In a less emotional sense, fear of the Lord is an acknowledgment that God is the source of all. It affirms that God makes a difference in the world. Thus it is the opposite of the fool's declaration that "there is no God" (Psalm 14:1), which, in the psalm, is not an atheistic declaration that God does not exist but an assertion that God is so far away that there is no reason to pay any attention to him. The scornful "there is no God" is an "I don't care" thrown in God's face. By contrast, fear of the Lord is a constant care about God, a constant awareness of God's presence.

Consequently, fear of the Lord is also an attitude of obedience to God's ways. Proverbs 2:5 and 2:9 set "the fear of the Lord" in parallel with "righteousness and justice and equity," which shows that fear of the Lord is expressed in doing what is right and good. An Old Testament prophecy that speaks ultimately of Jesus declares that he will "delight" in the fear of the Lord (Isaiah 11:3), an attitude illustrated by statements that follow: he will give just judgments for poor people (11:4) and will act rightly and faithfully (11:5). Biblical scholar Michael V. Fox points out that Psalm 34:11 "speaks of the fear of God as something that can be taught . . . and proceeds to inculcate certain principles: Avoid dishonesty; turn from evil; recognize God's omnipotence; know that God delivers the righteous and cuts off the wicked. These lessons belong to the content of 'fear of the Lord.'"

What is the connection between fear of the Lord and wisdom? Proverbs announces that "the fear of the Lord is the beginning of knowledge" (1:7). In other words, the combination of awareness of God and readiness to trust and obey him is the key to becoming wise; it is square one in the game of life. But we do not leave it behind as we make progress. It lies at the heart of wise living. The reason is that our wisdom, however great, is always severely limited. We can never fully grasp the mystery of our lives, for God orders events according to purposes hidden from our eyes (25:2). Thus while "the human mind may devise many plans," it is "the purpose of the Lord that will be established" (19:21; compare 16:9).

At one point, the sages' consciousness of the limits of human wisdom brings them close to canceling out their own attempts to gain wisdom in order to live well. Proverbs 20:24 declares: "All our steps are ordered by the Lord; how then can we understand our own ways?" Wisdom has to do with foreseeing consequences, thinking before we act. This proverb seems to undermine the whole attempt! It says that only God sees where we are going; indeed, God takes us wherever he wishes us to go. This comes close to saying that wisdom is impossible. Roland Murphy writes that this proverb contains "one of the most profound insights of the Bible. . . . On the one hand, there is human responsibility for one's actions . . . ; in fact, the whole thrust of the wisdom literature is to make one assume this responsibility. . . . On the other hand, God is the agent behind everything that occurs. The proverb emphasizes the mystery of it all by the addition of . . . a question that sounds as if it comes from the brink of despair, but it is really pointing out the limitations, and mystery, of wisdom." No wisdom that fails to take human limitations into account is truly wise. No amount of wisdom can so penetrate all the obscurities of life that it renders trust in God unnecessary.

Thus the sages advocate shrewdness and diligence, *so long as they are founded on fear of the Lord.* "Those who are attentive to a matter will prosper, and happy are those who trust in the Lord" (16:20).

Easier Said Than Done

Questions to Begin

15 minutes
Use a question or two to get warmed up for the reading. See also the questions on pages 25–27.

1 How much sleep do you need each night? How much do you get?

2 When have you made a purchase that seemed like a real bargain? Did it turn out to be such a good deal?

5 minutes
*Read the passage aloud. You may wish to ask participants to take
turns reading individual verses.*

The Reading: Proverbs 20

More Miscellaneous Proverbs

1 Wine is a mocker, strong drink a brawler,
    and whoever is led astray by it is not wise.
2 The dread anger of a king is like the growling of a lion;
    anyone who provokes him to anger forfeits life itself.
3 It is honorable to refrain from strife,
    but every fool is quick to quarrel.
4 The lazy person does not plow in season;
    harvest comes, and there is nothing to be found.
5 The purposes in the human mind are like deep water,
    but the intelligent will draw them out.
6 Many proclaim themselves loyal,
    but who can find one worthy of trust?
7 The righteous walk in integrity—
    happy are the children who follow them!
8 A king who sits on the throne of judgment
    winnows all evil with his eyes.
9 Who can say, "I have made my heart clean;
    I am pure from my sin"?
10 Diverse weights and diverse measures
    are both alike an abomination to the LORD.
11 Even children make themselves known by their acts,
    by whether what they do is pure and right.
12 The hearing ear and the seeing eye—
    the LORD has made them both.
13 Do not love sleep, or else you will come to poverty;
    open your eyes, and you will have plenty of bread.
14 "Bad, bad," says the buyer,
    then goes away and boasts.
15 There is gold, and abundance of costly stones;
    but the lips informed by knowledge are a
        precious jewel.
16 Take the garment of one who has given surety for
        a stranger;
    seize the pledge given as surety for foreigners.

17 Bread gained by deceit is sweet,
    but afterward the mouth will be full of gravel.
18 Plans are established by taking advice;
    wage war by following wise guidance.
19 A gossip reveals secrets;
    therefore do not associate with a babbler.
20 If you curse father or mother,
    your lamp will go out in utter darkness.
21 An estate quickly acquired in the beginning
    will not be blessed in the end.
22 Do not say, "I will repay evil";
    wait for the Lord, and he will help you.
23 Differing weights are an abomination to the Lord,
    and false scales are not good.
24 All our steps are ordered by the Lord;
    how then can we understand our own ways?
25 It is a snare for one to say rashly, "It is holy,"
    and begin to reflect only after making a vow.
26 A wise king winnows the wicked,
    and drives the wheel over them.
27 The human spirit is the lamp of the Lord,
    searching every inmost part.
28 Loyalty and faithfulness preserve the king,
    and his throne is upheld by righteousness.
29 The glory of youths is their strength,
    but the beauty of the aged is their gray hair.
30 Blows that wound cleanse away evil;
    beatings make clean the innermost parts.

10 minutes
Choose questions according to your interest and time. See also the questions on pages 25–27.

1 The proverb in 20:6 asks a rhetorical question. Does it imply that loyalty is rare—or nonexistent? The proverb in 20:9 asks the same kind of question. Is the answer "few" or "no one"?

2 What is meant by "diverse weights and diverse measures" in 20:10? (See also 20:23.)

3 In 20:18, what other endeavors could be substituted for "war"?

4 What is the logic behind 20:19?

5 Might "blows" and "beatings" in 20:30 be metaphors? For what?

A Guide to the Reading

If participants have not read this section already, read it aloud. Otherwise go on to "Questions for Application."

20:1. "Strong drink" is a "brawler"—the Hebrew word refers to roaring, growling, and barking. Perhaps the ancient Israelite party and concert scene could get as noisy as today's. Wisdom does not forbid drinking (9:5), just getting carried away.

20:3. It is honorable to refrain from "strife": more specifically the Hebrew refers to a *lawsuit.* Jesus and Paul took a similar view (Matthew 5:9, 25–26; 1 Corinthians 6:7).

20:5. From verse 5 through verse 17, many of the proverbs are variations on the theme of appearance versus reality. Surface impressions may be misleading (20:5, 10). People are not always what they claim to be (20:6). Pleasant things may turn out to be unpleasant in the long run (20:17). Therefore, skillful observation is required to determine what is real and important (20:15). Kings (20:8) are not the only ones who need to be careful observers of character; all of us need to be cautious in evaluating situations and people—and ourselves (20:9). Verse 12 reminds us of the source of the perceptiveness and discernment we need. (Verses 7, 13, and 16 do not seem to fit into this theme.)

20:7. The proverb does not speak explicitly of children who *imitate* righteous parents. It merely says that the children *after* the righteous will be blessed. Why would this be so? In any case, this is no ironclad law: compare Job 1:1–19; Jeremiah 31:29–30; Ezekiel 18:2–4.

20:9. Many proverbs speak of "the righteous." This one cautions us against putting ourselves in that category.

20:10. "Abomination," a strong term, expresses God's utter rejection of injustice (reinforced by 20:23).

20:11. This proverb seems to say that a child's behavior is evidence of the kind of adult he or she will become. Thus, early training is crucial (see 22:6). However, since the Hebrew verb translated "make known" also means "conceal," another translation is possible: "A child may be *dissembling* in his behavior, even though his actions are blameless and proper." In other words, a child may display behavior that pleases adults in order to conceal bad intentions. Thus, parents should not be fooled by a child's seemingly compliant behavior. Perhaps the proverb is deliberately ambiguous—the better to spur parents to pay careful attention!

20:14. Experienced wholesalers, sales reps, purchasing agents, and barterers in the bazaar all know that buyers and sellers do not show their hand to each other. But has the buyer here really scored a bargaining victory? Since boasting is often a sign of questionable achievement (25:14; 27:1–2), we may wonder.

20:15. Few if any proverbs indicate that wealth is desirable in itself. The motivation for becoming wise is to live long and well, not to have things. Compare 16:16.

20:16. The proverb speaker is not *recommending* harsh consequences for anyone who stands surety for a stranger. The proverb is a warning. If you guarantee a stranger's loan, you may end up hearing a judge say these dreadful words about you!

20:17. Quotation marks could be placed around the first half of this verse. It cites a view that the proverb writer does not share—and to which he adds a crucial observation ("afterward . . .").

20:21. It is hard to see what haste has to do with gaining an "estate," that is, an inheritance (although compare Luke 15:11–13). Another possible translation is "An inheritance *disdained* at the start will not be a blessing in the end." But the point of that statement is not exactly clear either.

20:22. Sometimes it is better to abandon the attempt to extract justice from an opponent (recall 20:3). The wise person lives with a sense of his or her limitations—and of God's providence (recall 3:5–8). Difficult advice!

20:24. On this proverb, see page 39.

20:25. This is a "look before you leap" proverb. To declare that something "is holy" is to donate it irrevocably to the temple for use in worship (see Mark 7:11–13).

20:27. Does this proverb mean that only God knows human beings, because he alone sees us from within? or that humans possess a God-given light, a self-awareness, that enables us to see into our own innermost depths? Perhaps both.

20:29. The very sign of older people's physical decline is their "beauty"—the Hebrew word means splendor, glory, majesty (see Psalms 29:4; 96:6). What an astonishingly positive view of old age! (Why is old age beautiful?)

20:30. Try reading this proverb in light of 3:11–12.

Questions for Application

40 minutes
Choose questions according to your interest and time. See also the questions on pages 25–27.

1 The insight in 20:5 could caution spouses (siblings, friends, workmates) against ascribing motives to each other. What other applications might this proverb have in these relationships?

2 Verse 13 targets excessive sleeping as an obstacle to getting on with life. What other activities—or "inactivities"—could be added to the list? Which do you tend to drift into?

3 Among people you know, to whom could you apply 20:15? What have you gained from them? How could you become more like them?

4 This same verse—20:15—expresses the conviction that material prosperity is not the ultimate criterion of the good life. From the readings so far in the book of Proverbs, what was the Israelite sages' picture of the good life? (There is no one simple answer.)

5 The king in 20:8 and 20:26 detects injustice and prevents the strong from exploiting the weak. How might this king be taken as a model for administrators, managers, supervisors, and others in positions of responsibility?

6 What past or present situation in your life comes to mind when you read 20:24? What effect has it had on your relationship with God?

7 In what situation might the observation in 20:25 be useful?

8 For personal reflection: When have you discovered the truth of 20:17? Do those experiences have something to teach you today?

Rash words are like sword thrusts, but the tongue of the wise brings healing.

Proverbs 12:18

Approach to Prayer

15 minutes
Use this approach—or create your own!

◆ Create a litany of intercession from the reading. For example, verse 1 might suggest "For all of us who struggle with addictions . . ." Verse 2 might suggest "For all political prisoners . . ." Verse 3: "For the times we are tempted to fly off the handle . . ." Go through the proverbs one at a time, letting participants take turns forming them into intercessory prayers, with the group completing each one by praying together: "Lord, have mercy." End with an Our Father and a Glory to the Father.

Saints in the Making

A Lovely Age

This section is a supplement for individual reading.

When I met Mary Nishimuta, she was working as a secretary while she underwent the process of separating from the religious order to which she had belonged for four decades. I would run into her at church-related events. She was always taking an interest in someone else and lending a hand with whatever needed doing. If there was cleanup to be done after a potluck dinner, Mary was in the kitchen at the sink. If there was a wedding, she was decorating the cake.

I learned that Mary had set her sights on serving Christ at an early age. That was why she joined the religious order as a teenager, and why she willingly worked for years as a maintenance supervisor for the order, even though she had no desire—or training—for the job.

Mary appeared to be a simple, even naive person. Yet there was steel behind her cheerful smile. Her order had not let her complete her high school education (in the eyes of her superiors, her Japanese ancestry marked her for menial tasks). As soon as she left the order, she got her diploma. A factor in her departure from the order was a conflict regarding the maintenance crew she was supervising at one of the order's elite high schools: Mary had been encouraging the workers to negotiate for higher wages.

Mary carried her approach to life with her into retirement. She became deeply concerned about the welfare of the unborn. When her pro-life activities once landed her in jail for a couple of days, she took her time there as an opportunity to make new friends—with whom she stayed in touch for years. The emblem of her later years, it seemed to me, was her strawberries. Every summer she would organize some much younger friends to go strawberry picking at farms in the area and then would take the young pickers door to door in the retirement home where she lived. This put a few pennies in the children's pockets and brought a little color into her neighbors' lives.

The sages tell us, literally, that "the splendor of old people is gray hair" (20:29). Mary Nishimuta helps me to see where the beauty of old age lies by illustrating the connection between this proverb and another one: "Gray hair is a crown of glory; it is gained in a righteous life" (16:31).

IF THE SHOE FITS . . .

Questions to Begin

15 minutes
Use a question or two to get warmed up for the reading. See also the questions on pages 25–27.

1 Did you like to play hide-and-seek as a child? What other games did you like to play?

2 What kind of music do you like to listen to when you're feeling down?

5 minutes
Read the passage aloud. Let individuals take turns reading subsections.

The Reading: Proverbs 25:2–28

Proverbs Mostly in Pairs

2 It is the glory of God to conceal things,
     but the glory of kings is to search things out.
3 Like the heavens for height, like the earth for depth,
     so the mind of kings is unsearchable.

4 Take away the dross from the silver,
     and the smith has material for a vessel;
5 take away the wicked from the presence of the king,
     and his throne will be established in righteousness.

6 Do not put yourself forward in the king's presence
     or stand in the place of the great;
7 for it is better to be told, "Come up here,"
     than to be put lower in the presence of a noble.

   What your eyes have seen
8   do not hastily bring into court;
   for what will you do in the end,
     when your neighbor puts you to shame?

9 Argue your case with your neighbor directly,
     and do not disclose another's secret;
10 or else someone who hears you will bring shame
          upon you,
     and your ill repute will have no end.

11 A word fitly spoken
     is like apples of gold in a setting of silver.
12 Like a gold ring or an ornament of gold
     is a wise rebuke to a listening ear.

13 Like the cold of snow in the time of harvest
     are faithful messengers to those who send them;
     they refresh the spirit of their masters.
14 Like clouds and wind without rain
     is one who boasts of a gift never given.

¹⁵ With patience a ruler may be persuaded,
   and a soft tongue can break bones.

¹⁶ If you have found honey, eat only enough for you,
   or else, having too much, you will vomit it.
¹⁷ Let your foot be seldom in your neighbor's house,
   otherwise the neighbor will become weary of you
      and hate you.

¹⁸ Like a war club, a sword, or a sharp arrow
   is one who bears false witness against a neighbor.
¹⁹ Like a bad tooth or a lame foot
   is trust in a faithless person in time of trouble.

²⁰ Like vinegar on a wound
   is one who sings songs to a heavy heart.
 Like a moth in clothing or a worm in wood,
   sorrow gnaws at the human heart.

²¹ If your enemies are hungry, give them bread to eat;
   and if they are thirsty, give them water to drink;
²² for you will heap coals of fire on their heads,
   and the LORD will reward you.

²³ The north wind produces rain,
   and a backbiting tongue, angry looks.
²⁴ It is better to live in a corner of the housetop
   than in a house shared with a contentious wife.

²⁵ Like cold water to a thirsty soul,
   so is good news from a far country.
²⁶ Like a muddied spring or a polluted fountain
   are the righteous who give way before the wicked.

²⁷ It is not good to eat much honey,
   or to seek honor on top of honor.
²⁸ Like a city breached, without walls,
   is one who lacks self-control.

10 minutes
Choose questions according to your interest and time. See also the questions on pages 25–27.

1 Reread 25:2–5 and look back to the proverbs dealing with kings in week 2 (14:35) and week 3 (20:2, 8, 26). What picture of kings and their responsibilities do these proverbs communicate?

2 Why is what 25:7 calls "better" better?

3 The proverb in 25:16 can be taken as a metaphor. What real-life applications could it have?

4 What kind of songs are meant in 25:20?

5 Why is a city that has lost its defensive outer wall (25:28) an apt image for a person without self-control?

A Guide to the Reading

If participants have not read this section already, read it aloud. Otherwise go on to "Questions for Application."

25:2–3. These two proverbs observe a scale of concealment. People may find it difficult to hide their secrets from kings; kings are better able to keep secrets from their people; but God can hide his secrets from everyone. God's plans are a total mystery to us— unless he chooses to reveal them (read this proverb as background to Ephesians 1:9 and surrounding verses).

    25:4–5. Dross is impurity removed from metal by refining. A ruler does well to get rid of his dross: bad officials and advisors. (What other kinds of dross should be removed from life to improve its quality?)

    25:6–7. Trying to get others to treat you as an important person can backfire. Fear of embarrassment may not seem like a very lofty motive for avoiding such behavior, but Jesus saw its usefulness (see Luke 14:7–11).

    25:7 (Beginning with "What your eyes have seen . . .") and 25:8. If the problem here is haste, the advice is Don't be quick to sue your neighbor; try to settle out of court. The problem, however, may be with the seeing. Thus: Don't go making accusations if you saw only part of what happened.

    25:9–10. The point here may be If you go to court against someone, be careful not to reveal a third party's secrets.

    25:11–12. The Hebrew of verse 11 is intriguing: it speaks literally of a word spoken "on its two wheels." Perhaps this means a "well-turned" phrase. But not only elegant statements are praised. A "rebuke" also is to be valued. Indeed, verse 12 suggests that a person's ears should be as receptive to a correction as they would be to a pair of lovely earrings.

    25:14. All smoke, no fire.

    25:15. The Hebrew term for "patience" here means staying calm and not losing your temper. Thus the proverb may have a positive meaning: Don't give in to anger and don't give up on trying to communicate; sweet reason may win the day. However, the word for "be persuaded" also means to be seduced, to let oneself be corrupted; it is related to a word for "fool"—a person who is naive and easily misled. So the proverb may have a negative meaning: A person who keeps his or her cool and keeps on talking may eventually break through the resistance of even a mature, responsible person and lead him or her to do something foolish. Seeing a TV commercial once may have no effect on you— but what about watching it a thousand times?

25:16–17. Lack of self-control is ever a problem. "Hate" here does not carry an emotional charge. The point is simply that your neighbor will not want to have anything to do with you.

25:20. Singing cheery songs to a sad person makes no more sense than taking off your coat on a cold day or pouring vinegar on a wound. In general, the proverbs are strongly optimistic: approach life energetically and use your head, and things will work out well. But the sages do not recommend giving glib encouragement. Sorrow may have depths that deserve respect (14:10). One who offers encouragement should keep 25:11 in mind.

25:21–22. Heaping burning coals on enemies' heads may refer to being generous with someone who steals from you and refusing to harm someone who strikes you (Matthew 5:39–42). Your refusing to return evil for evil may spur an enemy to reconsider his or her actions, to feel shame, to have a change of heart.

25:23. A problem here: in Israel and Palestine, northerly winds do not bring rain. No satisfactory explanation for this problem has been found. In any case, the second half of the verse is clear enough.

25:24. The sages were sensitive to the problem of nagging and argumentative wives: this proverb appears twice (21:9). It would be easy to compose a corresponding proverb about husbands. (Give it a try.)

25:25. Perhaps truly good news (of human generosity and heroism, of God's activity in the world), rather than breezy encouragements, is what the heavy-hearted person in verse 20 needs.

25:26. Psalm 55:22 promises that God will never permit the righteous to be "moved"—using the same Hebrew word here translated as "give way." Since God promises to support the just person, Roland Murphy observes, how cowardly it is for the just person to give way before the wicked. The issue is especially important when we are called on to take up the cause of those who cannot defend themselves against injustice (look ahead to 31:8–9).

25:27–28. Self-control! Self-control!

Questions for Application

40 minutes
Choose questions according to your interest and time. See also the questions on pages 25–27.

1   Reread 25:6–7. What are some modern strategies for gaining social recognition and being treated with deference? How are they to be evaluated from a Christian point of view? Consider Mark 10:35–45.

2   The sayings in 25:7–10 (beginning with "What your eyes have seen . . .") can be taken as advice about handling a dispute privately rather than dragging it out into the open. When have you seen the value of this approach? Do you always take it?

3   When have you been glad that you listened to someone's correction (25:12)? What have you learned about handling criticism well? What have you learned about giving it?

4 When have you been on the receiving end of 25:14? When could someone have quoted this proverb with regard to you? What have you learned from these experiences?

5 How could you put 25:21–22 into practice?

6 Identify the verses in this reading that deal with speech in some form. What view of the power and importance of speech, for good or ill, do the sages express? How seriously do you monitor what you say and the effects your words have on the people you speak with and about?

To make an apt answer is a joy to anyone, and a word in season, how good it is!

Proverbs 15:23

Approach to Prayer

15 minutes
Use this approach—or create your own!

♦ Begin with an Our Father. Then pray Psalm 37:1–19. This psalm is a prayerful meditation on God's support of those who trust him and try to follow his ways. If not everyone in the group has the same translation of the Bible, ask one person with a Bible to read the whole psalm aloud, slowly. End with a Glory to the Father.

This section is a supplement for individual reading.

A word fitly spoken is like apples of gold in a setting of silver" (25:11). The image is one of careful craftsmanship and charming effect. The golden apples ornament a piece of silver jewelry—perhaps a pin for fastening a cloak or a pendant adorning a woman's neck. The proverb seems to refer to a clever statement, a witty remark.

But there is more to this proverb than admiration for quick thinking and verbal skill. Gold and silver are weighty and valuable metals. The proverb expresses an appreciation for words that, like the gift of an expensive piece of jewelry, are costly to the giver and treasured by the recipient.

It is easy to believe that the costliest utterance many of us are in a position to deliver to someone is simply "Please forgive me"—perhaps followed by "I forgive you."

Two striking examples of speech that must have cost the speaker dearly recently came to my attention. In one incident, a teenager was driving home from a high school retreat with several friends. The weekend had been exhilarating, but everyone in the car was tired. The young driver briefly dozed off. Instantly, the vehicle veered off the road, flipped over, and crashed. The driver escaped serious injury, but not all the passengers did. One of them died. Soon after the funeral, the father of the child who died asked the young driver to visit him. In the course of their conversation, he told the young man, "I know what it's like to fall asleep at the wheel. Probably every driver does. What happened to you could have happened to me."

In the other incident, one young man shot and killed another young man in a drug-related crime. Afterward, the parents of the man who had been killed visited the parents of the man who was on trial for the murder. The message they brought was basically this: "We share your pain for your son, as we are sure you share our pain for ours."

In both these cases, people in the deepest mourning found in their grief something of great value to offer to others who were locked in their own pain. Their words were an expression of solidarity in suffering—more welcome, I suspect, than any piece of fashioned gold.

PRACTICE MAKES PERFECT

Questions to Begin

15 minutes
Use a question or two to get warmed up for the reading. See also the questions on pages 25–27.

1 What was the most unseasonable or surprising weather you ever experienced?

2 Do you like dogs or dislike them? Which kinds especially?

3 Do you like practical jokes? Describe a practical joke that amused—or did not amuse—you.

5 minutes
Read the passage aloud. You may wish to ask participants to take turns reading individual verses.

The Reading: Proverbs 26

On Foolishness, Laziness, and General, All-around Badness

1 Like snow in summer or rain in harvest,
   so honor is not fitting for a fool.
2 Like a sparrow in its flitting, like a swallow in its flying,
   an undeserved curse goes nowhere.
3 A whip for the horse, a bridle for the donkey,
   and a rod for the back of fools.
4 Do not answer fools according to their folly,
   or you will be a fool yourself.
5 Answer fools according to their folly,
   or they will be wise in their own eyes.
6 It is like cutting off one's foot and drinking down
      violence,
   to send a message by a fool.
7 The legs of a disabled person hang limp;
   so does a proverb in the mouth of a fool.
8 It is like binding a stone in a sling
   to give honor to a fool.
9 Like a thornbush brandished by the hand of a drunkard
   is a proverb in the mouth of a fool.
10 Like an archer who wounds everybody
   is one who hires a passing fool or drunkard.
11 Like a dog that returns to its vomit
   is a fool who reverts to his folly.
12 Do you see persons wise in their own eyes?
   There is more hope for fools than for them.
13 The lazy person says, "There is a lion in the road!
   There is a lion in the streets!"
14 As a door turns on its hinges,
   so does a lazy person in bed.
15 The lazy person buries a hand in the dish,
   and is too tired to bring it back to the mouth.
16 The lazy person is wiser in self-esteem
   than seven who can answer discreetly.
17 Like somebody who takes a passing dog by the ears
   is one who meddles in the quarrel of another.

¹⁸ Like a maniac who shoots deadly firebrands and
    arrows,
¹⁹ so is one who deceives a neighbor
    and says, "I am only joking!"
²⁰ For lack of wood the fire goes out,
    and where there is no whisperer, quarreling ceases.
²¹ As charcoal is to hot embers and wood to fire,
    so is a quarrelsome person for kindling strife.
²² The words of a whisperer are like delicious morsels;
    they go down into the inner parts of the body.
²³ Like the glaze covering an earthen vessel
    are smooth lips with an evil heart.
²⁴ An enemy dissembles in speaking
    while harboring deceit within;
²⁵ when an enemy speaks graciously, do not believe it,
    for there are seven abominations concealed within;
²⁶ though hatred is covered with guile,
    the enemy's wickedness will be exposed in the
    assembly.
²⁷ Whoever digs a pit will fall into it,
    and a stone will come back on the one who starts
    it rolling.
²⁸ A lying tongue hates its victims,
    and a flattering mouth works ruin.

10 minutes
Choose questions according to your interest and time. See also the questions on pages 25–27.

1 In 26:4–5, what does it mean to answer someone "according to their folly"?

2 What does the side-by-side placement of the proverbs in 26:4 and 26:5 imply about how proverbs should be used?

3 What might happen to a person who ties a stone into a sling (26:8)?

4 In addition to the problem for the dog, what other problem is there with taking a dog by the ears (26:17)?

5 What kind of pit does 26:27 seem to refer to?

6 How hopeful are the proverbs in chapter 26 about the possibility of foolish people becoming wise?

A Guide to the Reading

If participants have not read this section already, read it aloud. Otherwise go on to "Questions for Application."

26:2. Like a bird refusing to alight on an unsuitable branch, an unjustified curse declines to come down upon its object. Thus the curse has more sense than the curser—which makes the person who mindlessly shoots off curses against others look pretty dumb.

26:3. Are there people who just won't learn (compare 27:22)? Or is this proverb using shock rhetoric—exaggeration for the sake of effect—as a warning against acting foolishly?

26:4–5. The first proverb warns against getting into arguments that don't lead anyone to see anything more clearly and just get people more upset. Such arguments will make you look foolish (compare 29:9). The second proverb, however, concerns keeping a foolish person from the very worst kind of folly: being convinced that he or she is acting in a sensible manner. In addition, correcting a person who is mistaken may be helpful for other people in the situation (see the first half of 19:25)

26:7 and 26:9. Only a person who already has some wisdom knows whether and when and how a proverb might apply to a particular situation. (If you didn't have some common sense, what would you do with 26:4–5?) Verse 9 is ambiguous. Does the thornbush hurt the bystanders or the person who waves it around? Either way, as a nonbiblical proverb declares, a little knowledge is a dangerous thing. (Regarding 26:7: People in ancient cultures did not have our sensitivities regarding the disabled.)

26:10. For "hires," try substituting "puts in charge of a project," "entrusts a classroom to," "elects to public office." Placing an unqualified person in a position of responsibility is a disservice to everyone involved. Compare 26:6.

26:11. A fool repeats his or her mistakes as surely as a dog goes back to its mess. This gets at the essence of foolishness: failure to learn from one's mistakes. (I cannot refrain from mentioning that, in one of life's odd coincidences, just as I was writing this, my dog, Rupert, threw up on the carpet. Rupert, however, will not be given the opportunity to demonstrate the validity of the first half of this proverb!)

26:12. Trusting in wisdom is fine. Trusting in our *own* wisdom is dangerous. If we look within and see a wise person, we obviously have faulty eyesight, because none of us ever becomes completely wise. Therefore, an essential element of wisdom is the awareness that we still have a lot to learn. Tucked unobtrusively into a book designed as a training program in wisdom, this is a most significant proverb!

26:13. Exaggerating dangers may be a way of rationalizing inaction. A person who seems to have a fear problem may in fact have a laziness problem. Perhaps this proverb helps to explain why a homeowner in one of Jesus' parables accuses an apparently *timid* servant of *laziness* (Matthew 25:24–26).

26:16. A more literal translation helps to bring out the meaning of this proverb: "The lazy man is wiser in his own eyes than seven men who answer sensibly." Perhaps this proverb might pop into the mind of a physician dealing with a patient who is too lazy to make recommended changes in his or her diet.

26:17. This proverb and 25:26 offer contrasting advice about getting involved in another person's struggle for justice. (How can they work together to guide us?)

26:18–19. More literally, the practical jokester asks: "Aren't I a funny guy?" The proverbs show a low tolerance for pranks. Sensible people are too busy for such things. As verses 14–15 show, however, the sages were not humorless.

26:20–22. Yes, yes, gossiping is bad—and almost irresistible!

26:23. What kind of talk comes from "smooth lips"? In light of the preceding couple of proverbs, this one may refer to gossip and slander. Stories about other people's faults are entertaining, but the speaker and the listener engage in something "evil": taking pleasure in the unspoken assumption that "we're better." Or, in light of the following three proverbs, this one may warn us against letting ourselves be deceived by what other people say. Before acting on secret advice, it is best to bring it out for public discussion (26:26).

26:27. One who digs a pit to trap a neighbor (as one might dig a pit to trap an animal) will fall into it. Perhaps this proverb refers particularly to speech. Our slanders and lies have a way of coming back to haunt us.

Questions for Application

40 minutes
Choose questions according to your interest and time. See also the questions on pages 25–27.

1 Reread 26:1 and 26:8. What forms of honor and recognition are given to various kinds of foolishness in society today? What kinds of accomplishments often fail to receive sufficient honor?

2 When have you gotten into a useless argument with someone (26:4–5)? What have you learned about staying out of useless arguments?

3 When have you felt somewhat foolish for being in a position of responsibility that was more than you could handle? What did you learn from this experience?

4 When have you regretted acting on a partial insight or limited knowledge? What happened? Can this problem be avoided?

5 Reread 26:13. Have you ever, perhaps unconsciously, used fear of danger or fear of failure as a pretext for not making an effort? What other factors sometimes lie behind laziness?

6 Reread 26:24–26. What have you learned about how to determine whether a person is telling the truth?

7 For personal reflection: Recall a painful situation that taught you a lasting lesson. Are there other lessons you have learned from that situation that you have not put into practice? What is holding you back?

A fool takes no pleasure in understanding, but only in expressing personal opinion.

Proverbs 18:2

Approach to Prayer

15 minutes
Use this approach—or create your own!

◆ Reading the book of Proverbs leads us, sooner or later, to reflect on our shortcomings and sins. Pray Psalm 51, a prayer of repentance, in which the psalmist asks God to "teach me wisdom in my secret heart" (Psalm 51:6). If not everyone in the group has the same translation of the Bible, ask one person with a Bible to read the whole psalm aloud, slowly. End with a Glory to the Father.

A Living Tradition

Sadness about God

This section is a supplement for individual reading.

Several proverbs in chapter 26 poke fun at lazy people (26:13–16). Laziness has been the object of criticism by moral teachers through the centuries. In the Christian monastic tradition, laziness has received careful investigation.

Through long and patient efforts to grow in holiness and help others do the same, leaders in the monastic movement became convinced that laziness is sometimes rooted in a deeper problem. The monks identified this problem as a kind of sadness, which they called *sloth*—or *acedia,* from a Greek word meaning grief. Sloth, St. Thomas Aquinas wrote, is an "oppressive sorrow" that so weighs a person down that he or she wants to do nothing.

The monastic teachers observed that while this "oppressive sorrow" may lead a person into boredom and faint-heartedness, it may also drive him or her to aimless curiosity, excitement seeking, and idle talkativeness. Feeling too tired to make an effort and losing oneself in a frantic whirl of activity are, in the monastic analysis, two sides of a single dysfunctional coin.

The essence of sloth, Thomas wrote, is specifically sorrow in respect to God. The slothful person finds no joy in God. Naturally, the person who finds no joy in God is disinclined to try to love and obey him.

Where does this spiritual apathy come from? A possible source of sorrow with regard to God, Thomas suggests, is disparaging the gifts that God has given us to enable us to make our way toward him. Thomas also recognized that physical factors such as diet may play a part in sadness. (He perhaps would not be surprised by modern psychologists' discoveries of the somatic roots of many depressive disorders.) Nevertheless, at the heart of sloth lies a decision—a refusal to find joy in God and in the hope of being with him forever (see the *Catechism of the Catholic Church,* section 2094).

St. Thomas's remedy for sloth is not "Try harder! More discipline!" Rather, in view of the root problem—sadness about God—Thomas suggests that "the more we think about spiritual goods, the more pleasing they become to us, and forthwith sloth dies away." In other words, the more we turn our attention to the ways God has shown us his love, especially through his Son, the more we will experience his light scattering the darkness of our sorrow.

ALL'S WELL THAT ENDS WELL

Questions to Begin

5 minutes
Use a question or two to get warmed up for the reading. See also the questions on pages 25–27.

1 Who in your experience made an unusually wise choice of marriage partner?

2 Do you celebrate Mother's Day? If so, how?

5 minutes
Read the passage aloud. You may wish to ask participants to take turns reading individual verses.

The Reading: Proverbs 31

Mama Said . . .

1 The words of King Lemuel. An oracle that his mother taught him:
    2 No, my son! No, son of my womb!
      No, son of my vows!
    3 Do not give your strength to women,
      your ways to those who destroy kings.
    4 It is not for kings, O Lemuel,
      it is not for kings to drink wine,
      or for rulers to desire strong drink;
    5 or else they will drink and forget what has been decreed,
      and will pervert the rights of all the afflicted.
    6 Give strong drink to one who is perishing,
      and wine to those in bitter distress;
    7 let them drink and forget their poverty,
      and remember their misery no more.
    8 Speak out for those who cannot speak,
      for the rights of all the destitute.
    9 Speak out, judge righteously,
      defend the rights of the poor and needy.

A Woman Who Lives Well

    10 A capable wife who can find?
      She is far more precious than jewels.
    11 The heart of her husband trusts in her,
      and he will have no lack of gain.
    12 She does him good, and not harm,
      all the days of her life.
    13 She seeks wool and flax,
      and works with willing hands.
    14 She is like the ships of the merchant,
      she brings her food from far away.
    15 She rises while it is still night
      and provides food for her household
      and tasks for her servant-girls.

16 She considers a field and buys it;
   with the fruit of her hands she plants a vineyard.
17 She girds herself with strength,
   and makes her arms strong.
18 She perceives that her merchandise is profitable.
   Her lamp does not go out at night.
19 She puts her hands to the distaff,
   and her hands hold the spindle.
20 She opens her hand to the poor,
   and reaches out her hands to the needy.
21 She is not afraid for her household when it snows,
   for all her household are clothed in crimson.
22 She makes herself coverings;
   her clothing is fine linen and purple.
23 Her husband is known in the city gates,
   taking his seat among the elders of the land.
24 She makes linen garments and sells them;
   she supplies the merchant with sashes.
25 Strength and dignity are her clothing,
   and she laughs at the time to come.
26 She opens her mouth with wisdom,
   and the teaching of kindness is on her tongue.
27 She looks well to the ways of her household,
   and does not eat the bread of idleness.
28 Her children rise up and call her happy;
   her husband too, and he praises her:
29 "Many women have done excellently,
   but you surpass them all."
30 Charm is deceitful, and beauty is vain,
   but a woman who fears the LORD is to be praised.
31 Give her a share in the fruit of her hands,
   and let her works praise her in the city gates.

10 minutes
Choose questions according to your interest and time. See also the questions on pages 25–27.

1 Could the question in 31:10 be answered "Lemuel's dad"?

2 In the view of Lemuel's mother, what are a political ruler's responsibilities?

3 How early did the "capable wife's" servant girls begin their workday? Do you think they thought employment in this household was a good deal?

4 This superwife is physically robust (31:17). What elements of the description give an impression of her strength?

5 The description of the ideal wife ends with the declaration that she "fears the Lord" (31:30). In what way do her activities and attitudes (31:12–27) express fear of the Lord?

A Guide to the Reading

If participants have not read this section already, read it aloud. Otherwise go on to "Questions for Application."

31:1–9. At the end of a book in which a father has been teaching a son, this section offers welcome evidence that mothers too trained their children, even advising adult sons. It is also a reminder that wisdom is found not only within the traditions of Israel and the Church but in other places too. "King Lemuel. An oracle . . ." (31:1) may also be translated "King Lemuel of Massa," a region in northern Arabia. In any case, Lemuel is not an Israelite. These are instructions by a foreign woman to her son, a foreign king.

31:2–3. If the women to whom Lemuel's mother refers are those of his harem, this may be a warning not to let himself fall victim to palace intrigues.

31:6–9. I was reminded of these verses when a friend who is being overworked told me how his boss suggested that he relieve his panic attacks by going to a therapist and getting a prescription to help him relax! Alleviating a person's pain is fine, but it is no substitute for justice.

31:10–31. The Hebrew word translated "capable" (31:10) means powerful (including physically and sexually powerful—the same word is translated "strength" in verse 3), wealthy, brave, and socially prominent. The sage develops these various dimensions of strength in the portrait that follows. Here indeed is a *capable* woman! She seems to be a kind of superwoman—a mirage for the Israelite male. Who is she, really?

On one level, this woman is an ideal, although an attainable one. After all, at least one man found such a woman, for she is married. Because God is generous, a man might hope to find such a wife (see 18:22). This passage would provide an Israelite man with food for thought as he considered what qualities to look for in a potential spouse. Still, this woman seems more than any one woman could ever be.

In the opening chapters of Proverbs, wisdom is pictured as a woman (1:20–33; 9:1–6). Perhaps this woman also is an image of wisdom. Since the book is written in the form of instruction to a young man, this portrait at the end of the course suggests that if he listens to the sound teaching in the book and puts it into practice, he will become as happy as a man who marries a capable woman. The message to all of us is that if we make God's wisdom our life's companion, we will be as blessed as we would be if we made a stunningly wise choice of a marriage partner. Just as the husband of this wife would be happy to watch her exercising her talents in every corner of their life together, so should we let God's wisdom direct every aspect of our lives.

31:11. There is an air of physical strength about this woman. Indeed, she is subtly compared to a warrior and to a lion. Her husband will have no lack of "gain": the Hebrew word means "plunder." The "food" she supplies to her household (31:15) is, more literally, "prey."

31:14. The wife does not limit her business activities to the local and familiar but perceives opportunities in places strange and far away. She takes risks.

31:16. Not only does her vision range to far-off places; she also looks far into the future, making long-term plans and carrying them through to completion.

31:19–20. These two verses are tied together by the choice of words. In Hebrew the words for "hands" and "palms" are used twice: "She puts her *hands* . . . her *palms* hold . . . she opens her *palm* . . . reaches out her *hands*." The same Hebrew verb is used twice: literally she "*reaches out* her hands to the distaff . . . *reaches out* her hands to the needy." Thus the author shows the connection between the woman's economic activity (verse 19) and her care for the poor (verse 20). For this woman, labor literally goes hand in hand with generosity. She works hard *in order to* provide for others—not only for her own household but for her needy neighbors as well.

31:21. "Crimson" clothing would be fashionable but not necessarily warm. The Hebrew word, however, may also be read as "double," that is, double layers.

31:25. The woman is optimistic about the outcome of her efforts. Thus she is motivated to work hard—and freed to view the future with confident good humor.

31:26. Wisdom and kindness are placed side by side: kindness is the hallmark of true wisdom.

31:30. Fear of the Lord, the starting point for gaining wisdom (1:7), is also the crowning achievement of a life well lived.

Questions for Application

40 minutes
Choose questions according to your interest and time. See also the questions on pages 25–27.

1 How might the queen mother's admonition against escaping one's responsibilities for other people (31:4–5) apply outside the palace? What are your responsibilities to other people—family, friends, neighbors near and far? What kinds of escapism tend to distract you from your responsibilities? What sorts of things may lead you to ignore or forget the injustices that other people suffer (31:8–9)?

2 The queen mother advises her son to rule on behalf of the weak and needy, protecting them from oppression. Who fits this description of the weak and needy in today's world? What do her words say to those who rule in wealthy, powerful, democratic nations today (us, the voters!) about their responsibility to see that their nations act on behalf of people who are poor and oppressed?

3 In what ways is the capable wife of Proverbs 31:10–31 an unattainable ideal? In what ways is she a useful model for wives today? for husbands? In what ways is she not an entirely suitable model for women today? What does this "ode to a capable wife" have to say to those of us who are not married?

4 How has reading Proverbs affected your understanding of what it means to live well and make a success of your life? What is the most important insight that you are taking away from your exploration of Proverbs? the most important decision?

Pleasant words are like a honeycomb, sweetness to the soul and health to the body.

Proverbs 16:24

Approach to Prayer

15 minutes
Use one of these approaches—or create your own!

♦ In the spirit of Lemuel's mother's advice to him about ensuring justice for those who are poor and oppressed, pray Psalm 10, which is an appeal to God to give justice to those who are exploited by the powerful and wealthy. If not everyone in the group has the same translation of the Bible, ask one person with a Bible to read the whole psalm aloud, slowly. End with a Glory to the Father.

♦ Ask one participant to slowly read aloud this prayer from Proverbs 30:7–9. Pause for silent reflection. Close with an Our Father.

> Two things I ask of you;
>   do not deny them to me before
>   I die:
> Remove far from me falsehood
>   and lying;
>   give me neither poverty nor
>   riches;
>   feed me with the food that I
>   need,
> or I shall be full, and deny you,
>   and say, "Who is the LORD?"
> or I shall be poor, and steal,
>   and profane the name of my
>   God.

Saints in the Making

A Man Who Finally Spoke Out

This section is a supplement for individual reading.

"S peak out for those who cannot speak, for the rights of all the destitute" (31:8).

To many, Father Oscar Romero appeared to be a conservative and cautious person, hardly likely to become a public opponent of injustice in his native El Salvador. In the 1970s, fourteen families controlled more than half the cultivated land in the country, while about half the farm workers owned no land at all. But Romero tended to regard the ruling elite as sincere in their desire to foster a Catholic society. He was critical of those who called for radical change, partly because such efforts intensified divisions in society.

In 1974 Romero became the bishop of Usulután, a coffee-growing region. It was a time of worsening repression, with shadowy death squads striking down those who protested the conditions of the coffee workers. Bishop Romero complained privately to government authorities but did not voice any public criticism.

In February 1977, Romero was appointed archbishop of San Salvador, the capital city. In March, a right-wing death squad assassinated a friend of his, Father Rutilio Grande. The political murder of a priest was unheard of in Catholic El Salvador. The event was a turning point for the new archbishop. In weekly radio broadcasts, he began to publicize instances of torture and assassination perpetrated by government-supported death squads. He publicly denounced injustices toward the poor.

Criticized for dividing the nation, for meddling in affairs that were none of his business, for supporting Marxist revolutionaries, Romero responded that as a pastor he could not stand by silently while the government made war on its own people. At the same time, he urged those who opposed the government not to act "out of hatred or a desire for vengeance." He told those responsible for the repression, "I love you deeply. I am sorry for you because you go on the way to ruin." On March 24, 1980, an assassin killed Archbishop Romero as he celebrated Mass.

For a dozen years afterward, El Salvador was engulfed in a civil war that took the lives of some seventy-five thousand people. After 1992, the country achieved some degree of peace, with moderate political and economic improvements.

Looking on the Bright Side

How Could the Sages Be So Optimistic?

Every proverb makes a statement about the way the world is. A proverb is a tiny mirror, reflecting a fragment of reality—at least, reality as the proverb speaker sees it.

If we took all the proverbs in the book of Proverbs and pieced them together into one great, glittering mirror, what picture of the world would we see in it? What kind of world did the sages see?

We would not have to look for long into the proverbs' mirror of reality before a definite picture began to emerge. The proverbs themselves begin in chapter 10. That chapter alone presents multiple repetitions of a simple message: doing right leads to good results. In chapter 10 we find proverbs that tell us that upright, moral, responsible living "delivers from death" (10:2) and "prolongs life" (10:27; compare 10:16), is a "stronghold" (10:29; compare 10:9 and 10:25), grants desires (10:24), brings "blessings" (10:6), and "ends in gladness" (10:28). Chapter 10 sets the tone for the rest of the book. The proverb in 21:21 expresses the outlook well: "Whoever pursues righteousness and kindness will find life and honor."

In the sages' view, if you act wisely, work hard, and attend to your responsibilities to God and other people, you will enjoy prosperity, honor, and peace. "The Lord does not let the *righteous* go hungry. . . . The hand of the *diligent* makes rich. . . . The teaching of the *wise* is a fountain of life" (10:3, 4; 13:14; emphasis added).

The sages are convinced that the world is an orderly place, governed by an orderly God. Being sensible, diligent, and upright yields good results because that is the kind of world the wise, good God has created: a field in which good sowing leads naturally to an abundant harvest.

Of course, the sages are keenly aware that not everyone chooses to be wise, diligent, and upright. There is foolishness, laziness, and wickedness in the world—quite a bit, in fact, judging by the proverbs' frequent references to the dumb, the shiftless, and the bad.

Yet also in regard to fools, lazybones, and ill-intentioned people, the world displays its order—very much so. Painful results befall those who violate God's purposes. The world itself seems to operate as a just judge, rewarding good and punishing evil. The classic expression of this principle is found in 26:27: "Whoever digs a pit will fall into it, and a stone will come back on the one who starts it rolling." This proverb and others like it suggest that evildoing is a kind of boomerang that inexorably returns to inflict a fitting penalty on the wrongdoer. At other times, the proverbs speak of God more directly rewarding good behavior and punishing bad. Either way, those who act stupidly, refuse to work hard, and violate the moral order are sure to fail. That's how the world is. "One who walks in integrity will be safe, but whoever follows crooked ways will fall into the Pit" (28:18).

All of this raises an obvious question. Isn't it possible to find people of integrity who have not been preserved from oppression or catastrophe, as well as people who followed "crooked ways" but did not fall down any elevator shafts? The answer is painfully obvious—and so it must have been to the sages who composed Proverbs. How, then, can we explain the proverbs' reflection of a morally orderly world where good inevitably comes out ahead in the end? A couple of observations may help us understand this picture.

The first observation is that Proverbs is designed for training young people. Their moral development requires that they perceive the existence of a God-given moral order, reflected in creation. The teacher naturally seeks to lead them to see that right behavior is worthwhile. He or she puts the right road before the young and urges them to walk on it, with lessons from experience about the benefits of staying on the road and warnings about the dangers of getting off it. There may be darker paradoxes in earthly existence, but young people need to become committed to what is good and wise before they undertake to explore them. Only when the young have a solid moral foundation will they be able to examine the disorder in the world without their trust in God or their commitment to what is good being undermined.

The Bible itself contains profound critiques of the optimism reflected in Proverbs. The book of Job insists that the righteous do sometimes inexplicably suffer catastrophe. The book of Ecclesiastes insists that the wise do not always succeed—and that, in any case, earthly success brings no lasting satisfaction.

Neither Job himself nor the author of Ecclesiastes abandons wisdom and righteousness, even as they argue that the optimistic view of the world is only a partial account of how the world actually is. But these books are nevertheless critiques for the mature, shelved in the adult reading section of the biblical library.

The second observation is that the proverbs themselves show an awareness that the world is not quite so simple as 26:27 ("Whoever digs a pit will fall into it") by itself might suggest. For example, the statement "Better is a little with righteousness than large income with injustice" (16:8) acknowledges that doing right does not always yield desired material results (see also 16:19; 28:6). "Better is a little with the fear of the Lord than great treasure and trouble with it" (15:16) shows an awareness that sometimes we must choose to do right even when it does not mean gaining any earthly rewards.

Biblical scholar Michael V. Fox argues that the sages do not hold to any "mechanical" concept of reward and punishment. He points, for example, to 3:9–12:

Honor the LORD with your substance
> and with the first fruits of all your produce;
then your barns will be filled with plenty,
> and your vats will be bursting with wine. (3:9–10)

My child, do not despise the LORD's discipline
> or be weary of his reproof,
for the LORD reproves the one he loves,
> as a father the son in whom he delights. (3:11–12).

Fox writes: "The juxtaposition between 'faith and wealth' in 3:9–10 and 'faith and difficulty' in 3:11–12 is a paradigm of Proverbs' worldview. . . . The withholding of the promised benefits does not prove that a person is wicked or that God is unjust. Suffering as well as good fortune can flow from God's love."

Despite first impressions, on closer examination it becomes clear that the proverb writers do not claim to have discovered a cause-and-effect connection between wise living and a prosperous, satisfying life. The proverbs declare that there is a correlation between the two but stop far short of asserting the existence of any sort of law. Scholar James G. Williams observes that in the proverbs "there is a definite relation of deeds and consequence. . . . Such and such an attitude and pattern of behavior results *typically* (not always, not necessarily) in such and such an outcome." To show that the proverb writers do not claim to have discovered an unbreakable law of cause and effect in human life, Williams points to 23:9, which he translates: "Speak not in the ears of the senseless, for he will refuse the wisdom of your words." On this proverb, Williams writes:

One finds out why wisdom is refused, namely that the fool cannot assimilate wise words. But one does not learn that "senselessness" is caused in a strict sense, or that one should never speak to the foolish person because the result will always be the same (see 26:4–5). Such conclusions move beyond the range and intention of these proverbs. Indeed, the assertion, for example, "Whoever trusts in wealth will fall" [11:28—Williams's translation], could be called cause and effect thinking in one sense (Y is typically the result of X). But this is not a strict and hard determinism that holds "all X leads to Y" and "Y is always the result of X." This mental movement is practically never made in the wisdom tradition.

Thus, Williams remarks, the sages recognize that while "poverty may be the result of laziness (Proverbs 10:4) . . . there are poor people who are upright and rich ones who are crooked (Proverbs 19:1; 28:6)."

Certainly, the proverb writers have a sunny outlook. Their proverbs reflect a world that generally operates according to patterns of which an upright person may approve. But they know that the course of human events cannot be predicted. Creation exceeds our comprehension; it contains mysteries both marvelous and horrible (see 30:11–19). There *is* a God-given order in the world, the sages assert, and we may grow in understanding it and working with it. Yet they recognize, as Williams puts it, that "neither the world's secrets nor the divine reality can finally be comprehended."

Saving the Best till Last

Jesus, Speaker of Proverbs

J esus is famous for telling stories. The good Samaritan, the prodigal son, and the merchant who bought a "pearl of great price" are familiar not only to Christians but to many other people as well.

Jesus did not teach "except in parables," Mark tells us (Mark 4:34). By this Mark means that Jesus relied on little stories and simple images to communicate insights into the mysterious coming of God's kingdom. Yet in the Gospels the Greek word usually translated "parable" has additional meanings. In John's Gospel, *parable* refers to "figures of speech" (John 16:25). In some other Gospel passages, it refers to wise sayings or proverbs.

On one occasion, for example, Jesus took issue with the idea that eating certain kinds of food is displeasing to God. "There is nothing outside a person that by going in can defile, but the things that come out are what defile," Jesus explained (Mark 7:15). His disciples did not understand this statement, and so they went to him afterward and questioned him about this "parable" (Mark 7:17). On another occasion, when Jesus met opposition from his fellow townspeople in Nazareth, he said to them, "Doubtless you will quote to me this proverb, 'Doctor, cure yourself!'" (Luke 4:23). The Greek word translated "proverb" here is the same word usually translated "parable."

Jesus was a speaker of parables in the full sense of the Greek word, which basically means comparison and applies to all sorts of illustrations, analogies, riddles, and proverbs. Jesus is famous for his use of story parables. Although such parables were unusual in Jewish teaching in his day, they are one of the distinguishing characteristics of his ministry. Yet the Gospels portray him as being the master of the pithy saying as much as of the memorable story. If you open the Bible to the first of the Gospels— the Gospel of Matthew—and begin to read the first account of Jesus' teaching (the Sermon on the Mount—chapters 5–7), you will immediately find statements that sound very much like proverbs: "Blessed are the merciful, for they will receive mercy" (Matthew 5:7); "If salt has lost its taste, how can its saltiness be restored?" (Matthew 5:13); "A city built on a hill cannot be hid" (Matthew 5:14). The Sermon on the Mount is crowded with such little sayings.

In some cases, Jesus seems to use known proverbs in order to demonstrate the reasonableness of his teaching. For example, he winds up his instruction on trusting God with our material needs by telling his listeners, "Do not be anxious about tomorrow, for tomorrow will be anxious for itself. Let the day's own trouble be sufficient for the day" (Matthew 6:34, Revised Standard Version).

In other cases, Jesus seems to be coining new proverbs. (Scholars sometimes call these newly minted sayings of Jesus *aphorisms.*) "Do not swear by your head," Jesus advises, "for you cannot make one hair white or black" (Matthew 5:36). "Simply let your 'Yes' be 'Yes,' and your 'No,' 'No'" (Matthew 5:37—New International Version). "Do not let your left hand know what your right hand is doing" (Matthew 6:3). "Where your treasure is, there your heart will be also" (Matthew 6:21). What pungent statements! They surely stuck in the minds of Galilean peasants returning to their villages after listening to Jesus' outdoor preaching—and would reverberate in cultures East and West down through the centuries.

From the beginning to the end of his public life, Jesus spiced his teaching and conversation with familiar proverbs and original aphorisms. Even in his final hours, Jesus' facility for encapsulating a point did not desert him. As he was dragged out to the place of his execution, Jesus spoke briefly with some women along his route, ending his advice to them with a vivid warning of disaster about to befall Jerusalem: "If they do this when the wood is green, what will happen when it is dry?" (Luke 23:31).

In his skillful use and creation of proverbs, Jesus was a worthy successor of the earlier sages of Israel who composed the book of Proverbs. But how did the content of his proverbs compare with theirs?

Some of Jesus' sayings would fit so comfortably within the book of Proverbs that the reader has to check to make sure they are not actually quoted from that book. Jesus' declaration that "Every kingdom divided against itself is laid waste, and no city or house divided against itself will stand" (Matthew 12:25) perfectly reflects the outlook and even the two-part format of the proverbs in Proverbs.

Yet there are differences in outlook between the Old Testament proverbs and some of Jesus' proverbial sayings. The proverbs in the book of Proverbs focus on the present world; they recommend sensible and upright living as the path to prosperity, tranquillity, and genuine satisfaction in earthly life. Death stands at the horizon, beyond which the sages have only a shadowy sense of human existence. Jesus certainly does not devalue earthly life, but he opens up a view of eternal life in God's kingdom through resurrection from the dead, and he urges us to focus our attention on that life (see Matthew 6:19–21). The composers of Proverbs saw God's justice working itself out in events in this world. Jesus does not deny that there is a moral order in the present world or that God rewards and punishes even in this life; but again, he shifts our attention from the working out of God's justice in this world to the final execution of God's judgment in the age to come (see Matthew 5:3–12).

Absent from Jesus' proverbial statements—and from the rest of his teaching—are the assurances that wisdom and upright living will generally lead to well-being in this life and that foolishness and sin will generally lead to loss, disgrace, and early death. The books of Job and Qoheleth (Ecclesiastes) had subjected this view of earlier sages to a profound critique. Those works insisted that God's justice is not always and entirely worked out in this world; much suffering befalls the relatively innocent and much injustice goes uncorrected. Jesus seems to implicitly accept this criticism of the outlook in the book of Proverbs. (For Jesus' views, see, for example, Luke 13:1–5 and John 9:1–3).

In fact, much of Jesus' teaching communicates an expectation opposite that found in Proverbs. When Jesus declares, "All who exalt themselves will be humbled, and all who humble themselves will be exalted" (Matthew 23:12), he does not mean, as the proverb writers might have meant, that humble service to God will receive public recognition in earthly life. His point is that those who humbly trust and obey God, although they may not be "exalted" in this present world, may look forward to a greater exaltation and joy in God's kingdom.

Given his perspective on the present world and the age to come, Jesus does not counsel us to seek prosperity, well-being, and tranquillity in this present world. "What profit would there be for one to gain the whole world and forfeit his life?" Jesus demands (see Matthew 16:26). Instead, Jesus urges us to expend our resources—physical strength and well-being, talents, material resources—for the good of other people, in expectation of a condition of well-being in God's kingdom that far exceeds anything we might experience in the present world.

Jesus calls us to a deeper intimacy with God, and a closer imitation of God's love, than that which was envisioned by the Israelite sages. While the proverbs urge us to bear our responsibilities to others faithfully and even to treat strangers and enemies with kindness (see 25:21), Jesus goes further and calls us to "be merciful, just as your Father is merciful" (Luke 6:36). While the proverbs hold up a noble ideal of friendship (see 17:17), Jesus states, "No one has greater love than this, to lay down one's life for one's friends" (John 15:13).

If the wisdom of the book of Proverbs seems foolish to some (to those the book calls fools), the wisdom of Jesus may seem foolish even to many who would embrace the book of Proverbs. "Those who love their life lose it, and those who hate their life in this world will keep it for eternal life," Jesus declares (John 12:25), putting his outlook on life in a nutshell. He calls his followers to give him and his mission absolute priority, to the point of relinquishing possessions, even life (see Matthew 16:24–26; 19:16–24). Jesus' first followers found this approach to life almost incredibly challenging (see Matthew 16:21–23; 19:25). So does anyone who takes his teaching seriously today.

Yet the Gospel writers point us to the hidden reality of Jesus that makes his difficult teaching credible. He is the Son of God (Mark 1:1). He is God's personal Word, spoken to the human race (John 1:1–18). Jesus himself is the wisdom that enables us to live well, to make a success of our lives.

The metaphor that the book of Proverbs uses for God's wisdom is that of a beautiful, intelligent, strong, and capable woman who invites the seeker to dine at her table and live as her spouse. In the Gospels, this metaphor is exceeded in an astonishing way. Jesus of Nazareth *is* the wisdom for living that God offers to each of us. Jesus invites each of us to be his disciple, to learn his way of life by being with him. To get a life, follow him!

Proverbs of Jesus

Identifying proverbs in Jesus' teaching is not an exact science, primarily because it is not easy to define proverbs exactly. Whether a given statement is a proverb or not is somewhat in the eye of the beholder—or the ear of the hearer. But if proverbs are short, memorable statements about how the world works, how to live, and what is truly important in life, then the following statements seem to qualify. These are drawn from the Gospels of Matthew and John. Some are paralleled in the Gospels of Mark and Luke, which also contain a few proverb-like statements not found in either Matthew or John. What other statements of Jesus, from any of the Gospels, would you add to this list?

From Matthew's Gospel
"If salt has lost its taste, how can its saltiness be restored?" (5:13)
"A city built on a hill cannot be hid." (5:14)
"You cannot make one hair white or black." (5:36)
"Let your word be 'Yes, Yes' or 'No, No.'" (5:37)
"Do not let your left hand know what your right hand is doing." (6:3)
"Where your treasure is, there your heart will be also." (6:21)
"No one can serve two masters." (6:24)
"Is not life more than food, and the body more than clothing?" (6:25)
"Do not worry about tomorrow, for tomorrow will bring worries of its own. Today's trouble is enough for today." (6:34)
"Do not throw your pearls before swine." (7:6)
Beware of wolves in sheep's clothing (see 7:15).
"A good tree cannot bear bad fruit. . . . You will know them by their fruits." (7:18, 20; compare 12:33)
"Let the dead bury their own dead." (8:22)
"Those who are well have no need of a physician, but those who are sick." (9:12)
"New wine is put into fresh wineskins." (9:17)
"Be wise as serpents and innocent as doves." (10:16)
"Every kingdom divided against itself is laid waste, and no city or house divided against itself will stand." (12:25)
"Out of the abundance of the heart the mouth speaks." (12:34)
"Prophets are not without honor except in their own country and in their own house." (13:57)

"It is not what goes into the mouth that defiles a person, but it is what comes out of the mouth that defiles." (15:11)

"If one blind person guides another, both will fall into a pit." (15:14)

"It is not fair to take the children's food and throw it to the dogs." (15:26)

"What will it profit them if they gain the whole world but forfeit their life?" (16:26)

"Unless you change and become like children, you will never enter the kingdom of heaven." (18:3)

"Many are called, but few are chosen." (22:14)

"All who exalt themselves will be humbled, and all who humble themselves will be exalted." (23:12)

"First clean the inside of the cup, so that the outside also may become clean." (23:26)

"You always have the poor with you." (26:11)

"All who take the sword will perish by the sword." (26:52)

From John's Gospel

"Four months more, then comes the harvest." (4:35)

"One sows and another reaps." (4:37)

"It is the spirit that gives life; the flesh is useless." (6:63)

"Do not judge by appearances, but judge with right judgment." (7:24)

Let anyone who is without sin throw the first stone (see 8:7).

"The truth will make you free." (8:32)

"We must work . . . while it is day; night is coming when no one can work." (9:4)

"The one who enters by the gate is the shepherd of the sheep." (10:2)

"Unless a grain of wheat falls into the earth and dies, it remains just a single grain; but if it dies, it bears much fruit." (12:24)

"Those who love their life lose it, and those who hate their life in this world will keep it for eternal life." (12:25)

"Walk while you have the light." (12:35)

"Servants are not greater than their master." (13:16)

"No one has greater love than this, to lay down one's life for one's friends." (15:13)

"When a woman is in labor, she has pain. . . . But when her child is born, she no longer remembers the anguish." (16:21)

Like a camping trip, a Bible discussion group works best if you agree on where you're going and how you intend to get there. Many groups use their first meeting to talk over such questions and reach a consensus. Here is a checklist of issues, with bits of advice from people who have experience in Bible discussions. (A planning discussion will go more smoothly if the leaders have thought through the following issues beforehand.)

Agree on your purpose. Are you getting together to gain wisdom and direction for your lives? to finally get acquainted with the Bible? to support one another in following Christ? to encourage those who are exploring—or reexploring—the Church? for other reasons?

Agree on attitudes. For example: "We're all beginners here." "We're here to help one another understand and respond to God's word." "We're not here to offer counseling or direction to one another." "We want to read Scripture prayerfully." What do *you* wish to emphasize? Make it explicit!

Agree on ground rules. Barbara J. Fleischer, in her useful book *Facilitating for Growth,* recommends that a group clearly state its approach to the following:

- *Preparation.* Do we agree to read the material and prepare answers to the questions before each meeting?
- *Attendance.* What kind of priority will we give to our meetings?
- *Self-revelation.* Are we willing to help the others in the group gradually get to know us—our weaknesses as well as our strengths, our needs as well as our gifts?
- *Listening.* Will we commit ourselves to listening to one another?
- *Confidentiality.* Will we keep everything that is shared *with* the group *in* the group?
- *Discretion.* Will we refrain from sharing about the faults and sins of people who are not in the group?
- *Encouragement and support.* Will we give as well as receive?
- *Participation.* Will we give each person the time and opportunity to make a contribution?

You could probably take a pen and draw a circle around *listening* and *confidentiality.* Those two points are especially important.

The following items could be added to Fleischer's list:

♦ *Relationship with parish.* Is our group part of the adult faith-formation program? independent but operating with the express approval of the pastor? not a parish-based group?

♦ *New members.* Will we let new members join us once we have begun the six weeks of discussions?

Agree on housekeeping.

♦ *When will we meet?*

♦ *How often will we meet?* Meeting weekly or every other week is best if you can manage it. William Riley remarks, "Meetings once a month are too distant from each other for the threads of the last session not to be lost" *(The Bible Study Group: An Owner's Manual).*

♦ *How long will meetings run?*

♦ *Where will we meet?*

♦ *Is any setup needed?* Christine Dodd writes that "the problem with meeting in a place like a church hall is that it can be very soul-destroying," given the cold, impersonal feel of many church facilities. If you have to meet in a church facility, Dodd recommends doing something to make the area homey *(Making Scripture Work).*

♦ *Who will host the meetings?* Leaders and hosts are not necessarily the same people.

♦ *Will we have refreshments?* Who will provide them?

♦ *What about child care?* Most experienced leaders of Bible discussion groups discourage bringing infants or other children to adult Bible discussions.

Agree on leadership. You need someone to facilitate— to keep the discussion on track, to see that everyone has a chance to speak, to help the group stay on schedule. Rena Duff, editor of the newsletter *Sharing God's Word Today,* recommends having two or three people take turns leading the discussions.

It's okay if the leader is not an expert on the Bible. You have this booklet, and if questions come up that no one can answer, you can delegate a participant to do a little research between meetings. It's important for the leader to set an example of listening, to draw out the quieter members (and occasionally restrain the more vocal ones), to move the group on when it gets stuck, to remind the members of their agreements, and to summarize what the group is accomplishing.

Bible discussion is an opportunity to experience the fulfillment of Jesus' promise "Where two or three are gathered in my name, I am there among them" (Matthew 18:20). Put your discussion group in Jesus' hands. Pray for the guidance of the Spirit. And have a great time exploring God's word together!

Y ou can use this booklet just as well for individual study as for group discussion. While discussing the Bible with other people can be a rich experience, there are advantages to reading on your own. For example:

♦ You can focus on the points that interest you most.

♦ You can go at your own pace.

♦ You can be completely relaxed and unashamedly honest in your answers to all the questions, since you don't have to share them with anyone!

My suggestions for using this booklet on your own are these:

♦ Don't skip the Questions to Begin. The questions can help you as an individual reader warm up to the topic of the reading.

♦ Take your time on the Questions for Careful Reading and Questions for Application. While a group will probably not have enough time to work on all the questions, you can allow yourself the time to consider all of them if you are using the booklet by yourself.

♦ After reading the Guide to the Reading, go back and reread the Scripture text before answering the Questions for Application.

♦ Take the time to look up all the parenthetical Scripture references in the introduction, the Guides to the Readings, and the other material.

♦ Since you control the pace, give yourself plenty of opportunities to reflect on the meaning of Proverbs for you. Let your reading be an opportunity for these words to become God's words to you.

Bibles

The following editions of the Bible contain the full set of biblical books recognized by the Catholic Church, along with a great deal of useful explanatory material:
- The Catholic Study Bible (Oxford University Press), which uses the text of the New American Bible
- The Catholic Bible: Personal Study Edition (Oxford University Press), which also uses the text of the New American Bible
- The New Jerusalem Bible, the regular (not the reader's) edition (Doubleday)

Books

- Roland E. Murphy and Elizabeth Huwiler, *Proverbs, Ecclesiastes, Song of Songs,* New International Biblical Commentary (Peabody, Mass.: Hendrickson Publishers, 1999).

How has Scripture had an impact on your life? Was this booklet helpful to you in your study of the Bible? Please send comments, suggestions, and personal experiences to Kevin Perrotta, General Editor, Trade Editorial Department, Loyola Press, 3441 N. Ashland Ave., Chicago, IL 60657.

Notes

Notes